Y0-BDV-329

To
Vera and Allan Fraser

TREASURY of CANADIAN GLASS

Doris And Peter Unitt

CLOCK HOUSE

TREASURY OF CANADIAN GLASS

An Original Canadian Publication
First Edition - limited to one thousand copies (numbered)
Second Edition - December 1969

Published By

CLOCK HOUSE PUBLICATIONS Rgd.

Clock House - 711 Water St. - Peterborough - Ontario - Canada
© *Copyright 1969 Clock House Publications*

ALL RIGHTS RESERVED

No part of this book may be reproduced in any form without permission in writing from the publishers, except by a reviewer who may quote brief passages in a review to be printed in a newspaper or magazine.

Printed in Canada by

MAXWELL REVIEW Ltd., *Peterborough, Ontario*
Printed by lithography on Paragon Offset Brilliant 200M stock.
Text is 10pt. Galaxy, heads are Bodoni Bold Italics.

Frontispiece and Dust Jacket

CANADIAN GLASS IN COLOUR
Clear (flint) Water Pitcher white opal "lattice" design. Burlington Glass Works.

FOURTH PRINTING

Instead of
a piece of pillar
love to Donna
Christmas
1973
Slim

TREASURY OF CANADIAN GLASS

ACKNOWLEDGEMENTS

The authors wish to thank all those who assisted in the preparation of this book. Our thanks go to

The Honourable James Auld, Ontario.

Peter Behn, Toronto.

Marian and Douglas Bird, Orillia.

Laurette and Ivor Brown, Orillia.

Mabel and Arthur Burridge, Pleasant Point.

Lovinia Byington, Portland.

Paul Byington, Portland.

Mabel and Cardiff Cline, St. Mary's.

Agatha and John Cornacchia, Barrie.

Gene Cornacchia, Barrie.

Mildred and Joe Creech, St. Mary's.

Jacqui and Dr. Wm. Davis, St. Mary's.

Gertrude and Lorne Durward, London.

Melva Ecker, Exeter.

Vera and Allan Fraser, Exeter

Ardys Glenn, Exeter.

Elisha and George Hicks, Listowel.

W. Higgins, Truro, Nova Scotia.

Janet Holmes, Royal Ontario Museum, Toronto.

George MacLaren, Nova Scotia Museum, Halifax.

Rita and Alan Markham, Toronto.

Irene and Frank Markvart, Trenton.

Helen and Russ McLaren, Oro.

Faye and Ed McLean, London.

Beth McMaster, Lakefield.

Willa and Harold Mercer, Orillia.

Eunice and Frank Millard, Peterborough.

Betty and Jim Milligan, Orillia.

Earl Morris, Napanee.

Peter Myers, Barrie.

Jenny & S. "Tiger" Norton, Millbrook.

Paula and John Pearson, Vandorf.

Mrs. Edna Renwick, Lakefield.

John R. Sheeler, Toronto.

Lena Stanbury, Agincourt.

Myrtle and Bert Wannamaker, Foxboro.

Mr. Donald Webster, Royal Ontario Museum.

Mr. and Mrs. Eric Wilson, Peterborough.

Charles H. Williamson, Omemee.

The Honourable John Yaremko.

In making available their collections for photographing, loaning pertinent documents and providing essential information they made the work of preparation a pleasure.

We would also like to convey our appreciation to The Royal Ontario Museum and The Nova Scotia Museum for making the Canadian Glass Collections available for photographing.

To Peter LaBranche - President, Max Glover, Production and Art Sanders (Special Projects) Maxwell Review Printers - Peterborough.

Barry Hum, Student help, Peterborough.

Jock Mitchell, Who helped design then built our lightbox, thus enabling us to take our studio to the glass and provide hundreds of photographs which would otherwise have been unobtainable.

Sandy Stewart - Peterborough.

Rosemary Unitt, Our Secretary.

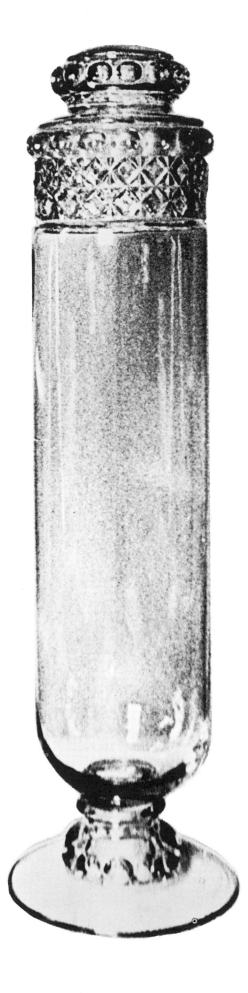

CONTENTS

BURLINGTON PITCHER WITH GOBLET (Etched)

AUTHOR'S PREFACE

The "**Treasury of Canadian Glass**" has been compiled to fill a need. It is designed to give the student and collector of glass information regarding the **pattern and form** of those pieces considered Canadian. To identify a pattern it is useful to know the shape of the foot, finial and handle as well as seeing how the design can vary according to the form in which it is made. Although the same pattern was made in several factories there would be some differences in the wares produced. Glass makers were individualists and added a personal touch to their work. This book shows many of the forms and the patterns which up to June of 1969 were considered to have originated or to have been manufactured in Canada.

It has not been possible to show every form seen or use every photograph taken. The collector can be sure however if a butter dish is shown that pattern was made in a four-piece setting and most likely several other forms. If a pitcher is included then tumblers were usually made. It seems that goblets were not always part of a set and some patterns turn up in goblet form only .

Our selection of coloured pieces will help to illustrate the fact that Canadian Glass equals in beauty of form and quality the much sought after Art Glass from other countries.

Fascinating stories have been told of the origin of glass and no one knows exactly where the first was made. Glass beads dating from 2500 B.C. from Egypt and a green glass rod from Eshnunna in Babylonia circa 2600 B.C. are known. It is without doubt that glass vessels of Egyptian origin were made from 1448 B.C. onwards. The method of making was to first form a clay shape fixed to a metal rod which was dipped into molten glass, first a layer of opaque blue glass, then coils of glass thread were looped around. A comb-like instrument was used to feather, zigzag or arcade the threads. Colours included, sealing-wax red, yellow, green and white. Some pieces had the colours rolled (marvered) in making the surface of the vessel completely smooth. To other pieces handles - usually of translucent glass were added, a few have been found with patterned "canes". Glass vessels at this time were quite small and used in the main to contain salves, perfumes and oils.

Decorating with a lapidary's wheel was another form of ornamentation.

Glass making in the Americas dates from 1535. Puebla de los Angeles in Mexico being the first site and the first glasshouse was situated in the town of C'ordoba del Tucuman, Argentina. Cullet was remelted and fashioned into vessels, and thick, semi-transparent sheets of glass.

Jamestown was the centre chosen by **The London Company of Virginia** to establish a glasshouse for the making of "Glasses" and beads in the year 1608. During the winter of 1609 disaster in form of starvation wiped out 440 of the 500 inhabitants. A second attempt was planned in 1621 but this also failed. Excavation of the site proved that considerable quantities of glass had been melted there, but no evidence of bead making was found.

It was not until a century later that glass making began to take a proper hold and the ups and downs of the industry have provided material for many books.

The story of glass making in Canada is short in comparison to that of other glass producing countries, and yet perhaps not as short as we have come to believe. In "A Guide to Early Canadian Glass" by Hilda and Kevin Spence mention is made of medicine vials of the period prior to 1787. A photograph (plate 1) shows how fragile they were. The origin of these vials is not proven, but it is possible that they were the first Canadian made glass containers.

More and more research is being done and hundreds of enthusiasts are tracking down clues, searching for information, seeking to prove or disprove accepted stories, hunting for old catalogues, spending hours and hours in archives, looking up patents, scrutinizing micro-films of early newspapers and documents happy if they find one more undisputable fact to add to the total story of Canadian Glass.

Many of the people engaged in the research of Canadian glass are members of "Glassfax", an organization sponsored by the Dominion Glass Company Limited. Other researchers are assisted by the Government and Provincial Museum authorities, the sponsorship of "Digs" is doing a great deal to provide positive proof of patterns or articles made in Canadian Glassworks. There is much to be added to the story of Canadian Glass and every book is but a stepping stone to the others that must follow.

Doris and Peter Unitt
Peterborough, Canada

July 1st, 1969

GLASS FACTORIES OF CANADA

ALBERTA
The Dominion Glass Company Ltd., REDCLIFF   (1913 - ?)
BRITISH COLUMBIA
The Crystal Glass Company, NEW WESTMINISTER   (1907 - 1908)
MANITOBA
The Manitoba Glass Company Limited, BEAUSEJOUR   (1907 - 1914)
The Dominion Glass Company Limited, BEAUSEJOUR   (1913 - 1918)
NEW BRUNSWICK
The New Brunswick Crystal Glass Company,
                        EAST SAINT JOHN   (1874 - 1878)
The Humphreys Glass Works, MONCTON   (1915 - 1920)
NOVA SCOTIA
The Nova Scotia (Diamond) Glass Company, TRENTON   (1881 - 1892)
The Humphreys Glass Works, TRENTON   (1890 - 1914)
The Lamont (Diamond) Glass Company,
                 TRENTON and NEW GLASGOW   (1890 - 1902)
ONTARIO
The Mallorytown Glass Works, MALLORYTOWN   (   )
                                  (closed 1839 - 1840)
The Hamilton Glass Works, HAMILTON   (1865 - 1895)
The Burlington Glass Works, HAMILTON   (1875 - 1909)
The Napanee Glass Works, NAPANEE   (1881 - 1883)
The Toronto Glass Company, TORONTO   (1894 - 1900)
            PARKDALE 1900-1913; DOMINION 1913 - 1920)
The Sydenham (Dominion) Glass Company,
                        WALLACEBURG   (1895 -   )
The Erie Glass Company, PORT COLBORNE   (c.1893 - c.1898)
The Foster Glass Works, PORT COLBORNE   (1895 - 1899)
The Ontario Glass Company, KINGSVILLE   (1899 - 1902)
The Jefferson (Dominion) Glass Company, TORONTO   (1913 - 1925)
QUEBEC
The Ottawa Glass Works, COMO   (c.1847 - ?)
The Canada Glass Company, HUDSON   (c.1865 - 1875)
John C. Spence, MONTREAL   (1845 - 1867)

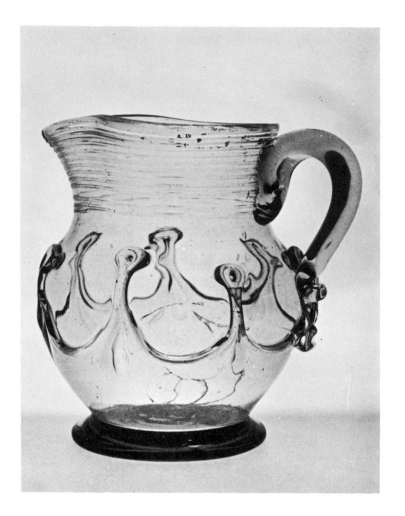

EARLY CANADIAN GLASS

1. *Mallory pitcher on display at Royal Ontario Museum.*

2. *Swan Whimsey.*

3. *Duck Whimsey, believed to be Wallaceburg.*

4. *Mallory bowl.*

GLASS FACTORIES (continued)

The Foster Brothers Glass Works, ST. JOHNS	(1855 - 1875)
The St. Lawrence Company, MONTREAL	(1867 - 1875)
The St. Johns Glass Company, ST. JOHNS	(1875 - 1878)
The Excelsior Glass Company, ST. JOHNS	(1878 - 1880)
The Excelsior Glass Co. MONTREAL	(1880 - 1883)
The North American Glass Company, MONTREAL	(1883 - 1890)
The (early) Dominion Glass Company, (MONTREAL)	(1886 - 1898)
The Diamond Flint Glass Company Limited, MONTREAL	(1903 - 1913)
The Dominion Glass Company Limited, MONTREAL	(1913 - ?)
The Consumers Glass Company Limited, MONTREAL	(1913 - ?)
The Demarais and Robitaille Limited Glass Company, MONTREAL	(1924 - 1925)

THE SEQUENCE OF GLASS WORKS THAT LED TO THE FORMATION OF THE PRESENT DOMINION GLASS WORKS

Foster Brothers Glass Works, St. Johns, P.Q.	1855 - 1875
St. Johns Glass Co., St. Johns	1875 - 1878
Excelsior Glass Co., St. Johns	1878 - 1880
Excelsior Glass Co., Montreal	1880 - 1883
North American Glass Co., Montreal	1891 - 1902
Diamond Glass Co., Montreal	1903 - 1913
Dominion Glass Co., Montreal and elsewhere	1913 - still operating

CANADIAN COMPANIES THAT BECAME PART OF DOMINION GLASS COMPANY (MOST OF THEM DURING THE DIAMOND GLASS STAGE)

The (early) Dominion Glass Co., Montreal	1886 - 1898
Hamilton Glass Works, Hamilton, Ontario	1865 - 1895
Toronto Glass Co., Toronto	1894 - 1900
Parkdale	1900 - 1913
Sydenham Glass Co., Wallaceburg, Ontario	1895 - 1913
Independent Producers Co., Ltd., Toronto, Ontario	? - 1912

Jefferson Glass Co., a branch of the Jefferson Glass Co. of Follansbee, West Virginia. Took over (purchased) Independent Producers Co. Ltd. Glassworks in Toronto, Ontario, 1912. (controlled by Dominion after 1913, closed in 1925).

The Nova Scotia Glass Co., Trenton, N.S.	1881 - 1892
(joined Diamond Glass Co. in 1890, closed in 1892.)	
Lamont Glass Co., Trenton, N.S.	1890 - 1902
(joined Diamond in 1898 and closed in 1902.)	
Dominion Glass Co., Redcliff, Alberta	1913 - still operating
Manitoba Glass Co., Beausejour, Man.	1907 - 1914
Taken over by Dominion	1913 - 1918

BURLINGTON PITCHERS

MARY GARDINER TYPE

DIAMOND SUNBURST

ROSE RED & PINK ON CLEAR

TREE OF LIFE - CLEAR TO CREAM
TO YELLOW OPAL

GLASS COMPANIES NOT RELATED TO DOMINION

QUEBEC

Masson & Co., Como, P.Q.	1846 - 1847
Ottawa Glass Works, Como, P.Q.	1847 - 1848
Canada Glass Works, Como, P.Q.	1849 - 1875
John C. Spence, Montreal	1854 - 1867
British-American Glass Co., Hudson, P.Q.	1855 - 1860
Montreal Glass Co., Hudson, P.Q.	1860 - 1865
(joined Canada Glass Co. in 1865, closed in 1875)	
St. Lawrence Glass Co., Montreal	1867 - 1875
Demarais & Robitaille Ltd., Montreal	1924 - 1925
Consumers Glass Co., Montreal later Toronto	1913 - still operating

ONTARIO

Mallorytown Glass Works, Mallorytown, Ont.	
(first Canadian company operated.)	
from date unknown - closed	1839 - 1840
Burlington Glass Works, Burlington, Ont.	1875 - 1909
Glass Bros. & Co., London, Ontario (potters)	circa 1882 - 1890
Napanee Glass Works, Napanee, Ont.	1881 - 1883
Erie Glass Co., Port Colborne, Ont.	1893 - 1898
Foster Glass Works, Port Colborne, Ont.	1895 - 1899
Ontario Glass Co., Kingsville, Ont.	1899 - 1902

NOVA SCOTIA AND NEW BRUNSWICK

Humphreys Glass Works, Trenton, N.S.	1890 - 1914
Moncton, N.B.	1915 - 1920
The New Brunswick Crystal Glass Co., East St. John, N.B.	1874 - 1878

BRITISH COLUMBIA

Midwest Glass Co., New Westminister, B.C.	1929 - 1931
The Crystal Glass Co., New Westminster, B.C.	1907 - 1908

SEALERS OR FRUIT JARS — CANADIAN MANUFACTURERS

COMPANY

Excelsior Glass Co., St. Johns	1878 - 1880
Montreal	1880 - 1883
North American Glass Co., Montreal	1883 - 1891
Diamond Glass Co., Montreal	1902 - 1913
The (early) Dominion Glass Co., Montreal	1886 - 1898
Dominion Glass Co., Montreal and elsewhere	1913 - present
Hamilton Glass Works, Hamilton, Ont.	1865 - 1895
Sydenham Glass Co., Wallaceburg, Ont.	1895 - 1913
Burlington Glass Works, Hamilton, Ont.	1875 - 1909
Midwest Glass Co., Winnipeg, Manitoba	1919 - 1931
Ontario Glass Co., Kingsville, Ont.	1899 - 1902
Sager Glass Corp. Ltd., Toronto	
Consumers Glass Co., Montreal and later Toronto	1913 - present
Glass Bros. & Co. (potters), London, Ont. & Brantford, Ont.	1882 - 1890

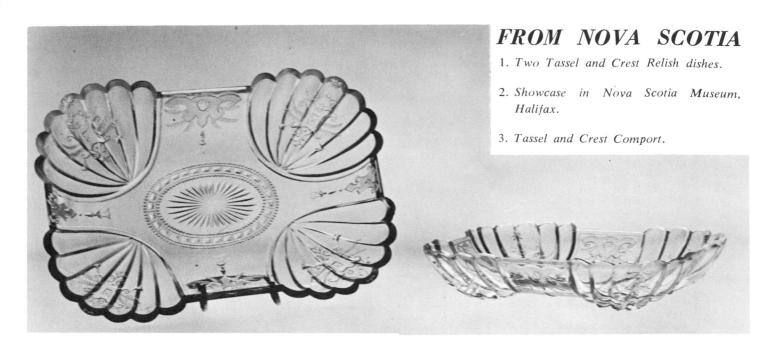

REFERENCES AND ABBREVIATIONS

NORTH AMERICAN FRUIT JAR INDEX   Marion and Douglas Bird
Bird, Fruit Jar Index

NOVA SCOTIA GLASS   George MacLaren
MacLaren, Nova Scotia Glass

BEAUSEJOUR'S GLASS WORKS   Max Provick
Provick, Beausejour's Glass Works

EARLY CANADIAN GLASS   Gerald Stevens
Stevens, Early Canadian Glass

EARLY ONTARIO GLASS   Gerald Stevens
Stevens, Early Ontario Glass

IN A CANADIAN ATTIC   Gerald Stevens
Stevens, Canadian Attic

CANADIAN GLASS 1825-1925   Gerald Stevens
Stevens, Canadian Glass 1825-1925

THE BURLINGTON GLASS SITE   John R. Sheeler
Sheeler, Burlington Glass Site

A GUIDE TO EARLY CANADIAN GLASS   Hilda & Kevin Spence
Spence, Early Canadian Glass

EARLY AMERICAN PATTERN GLASS   Ruth Webb Lee
Lee, American Pattern Glass

VICTORIAN GLASS   Ruth Webb Lee
Lee, Victorian Glass

GOBLETS — BOOKS 1 & 2   Dr. S. T. Millard
Millard, book one or Millard, book two

AMERICAN GLASS   George & Helen McKearin
McKearin, American Glass

AMERICAN PRESSED GLASS & FIGURE BOTTLES   Albert Christian Revi
Revi, American Pressed Glass

A HERITAGE OF LIGHT   Loris S. Russell
Russell, Heritage of Light

KAMM-WOOD ENCYCLOPEDIA OF AMERICAN
PATTERN GLASS   Vol. I and II
Kamm-Wood Book One or Kamm-Wood Book Two

CANADIAN GLASS — A FOOTNOTE TO HISTORY   Edith Chown Pierce
Pierce, Canadian Glass

SALT SHAKERS   Dr. Arthur Peterson
Peterson, Shakers

THE BOTTLE COLLECTOR   Azor Vienneau
Vienneau, Bottle Collector

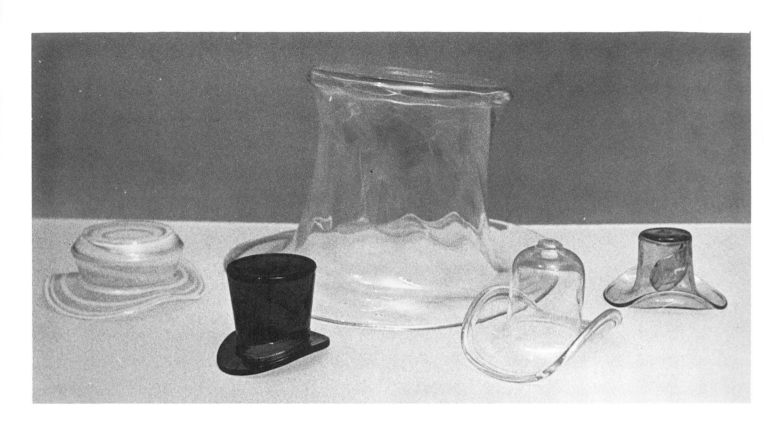

CANADIAN WHIMSEYS

1. *A Variety of hats — Ontario.*
2. *Cornucopias — Blue & Amethyst*

CANADIAN GLASS PATTERNS

The names used for patterns will be those used by Gerald Stevens in **Canadian Glass c. 1825-1925** and George MacLaren in **Nova Scotia Glass,** Occasional Paper No. 4 Historical Series No. 1 (revised).

Any patterns which have been listed in **Canadian (antique) Collector"** articles. **"The Burlington Glass Site"** will have those pattern names used by John R. Sheeler. Where any confusion of name occurs the name selected by the quoted authority will be used first and the name commonly used included on the pattern page.

For example, **Nova Scotia Crown** is referred to as **Pillar** by Ontario Collectors and **Honeycomb** is the more popular reference to that pattern actually catalogued as **New York.** A pattern which previously had neither name nor number is now known as **Feather Band** and documentation that the design was used by Dominion Glass Company Limited found in an early catalogue. See Stevens **Canadian Glass 1825-1925,** page 150.

If a pattern has been previously listed as the product of an America Glasshouse or houses reference will be given and any other nomenclature it may have had will be included. Since research has proved that a number of patterns were made in several factories across Canada as well as in the American factories, it is not surprising that collectors wonder what can be considered Canadian and what can not.

Possibly the answer should be: if the pattern is known to have been produced in any of the Canadian Factories, does not bear the mark of an American or English maker and is of a quality of glass similar to other proven pieces of Canadian origin it can be accepted as Canadian.

The popular **Thistle** design was also manufactured by the Highbee Glass Company of the United States but the pieces from that factory have the raised figure of a honey bee enclosing the letters H. I. G.

Gerald Stevens states that Canadian tablewares were not identified by any mark whatsoever.

CANADIAN ETCHED GLASS

CANADIAN GLASS PATTERNS

ACADIAN
> See Nova Scotia Acadian.

AEGIS
> This pattern is known to various American authorities. Lee, **"Victorian Glass"** page 79. Millard, **Book two,** page 82. Kamm-Wood **Book one,** page 60 gives it another name — **Bead and Bar Medallion** Canadian attribution. Spence, **Early Canadian Glass,** page 105. This attribution confirmed by the finding of shards at the series of 'private digs' on the Burlington Glass Site during the year 1967. A dish of this pattern on display at the Royal Ontario Museum, Toronto.

AE.V BAND
> Pitcher with Burlington marks.

AMERICAN
> A design for lamp base, pages 110/112 Steven's **"Canadian Glass 1825/1925"** Diamond Glass Co.; Montreal.

ANDERSON
> A pattern by this name is mentioned by Revi, **American Pressed Glass and Figure Bottles,** page 276. Not illustrated. Made by O'Hara Glass Company Ltd. Known as their No. 82 pattern. **Arrowhead** Kamm-Wood **Book one.** Page 18. Canadian Attribution by Sheeler, **"Burlington Glass Site"** Canadian (antiques) Collector. January, 1969.

ARGYLE
> See Squared Daisy and Diamond.

ARROWHEAD
> See Anderson.

ARROWHEAD IN OVAL
> See Beaded Oval Fan #2.

ATHENIAN
> Authenticated by Stevens **"Canadian Glass 1825/1925"** (Catalogue No. 6. Dominion Glass Company Limited, Montreal) Page 125. Shown in Spence **"Early Canadian Glass"** page 82/83 under the name of **"Palm and Diamond Point"**. Not to be confused with **"Anthemion"** shown on plate 58. Lee, **"Early American Pressed Glass"**.

BAR AND FINE CUT
> See Nova Scotia Diamond Ray.

BARS AND SQUARES
> See Nova Scotia Centennial.

BEAD AND BAR MEDALLION
> See Aegis.

BEAD AND PETAL
> (The No. 210 Pattern) Authenticated by Stevens **Canadian Glass 1825/1925** pages 113 and 129 made by Diamond Flint Glass Company Ltd., Montreal Works. Shown in Spence, **"Early Canadian Glass"** Pages 87/89 with the information that Mrs. Robinson of Toronto, one of the outstanding authorities on Canadian glass, had traced it to the Jefferson Glass Co; Toronto. The pattern appears in Dominion Glass Company Limited catalogue and also in Jefferson Glass Company Limited Catalogue No. 21. **Crocus** is a name suggested in the Spence book.

ETCHED TUMBLERS   *(LAMONT GLASS WORKS, N.S.)*

BEADED ARCH

Attributed as Canadian by Spence "Early Canadian Glass" page 99 and listed as "Chain" Lee, **Early American Pressed Glass**, plate 132, shows an entirely different pattern under that name. Metz **Book one,** page 190-191 shows the pattern as **Beaded Arched Panels** and lists "Only goblet Canadian authentication established at "Burlington dig". Cream pitcher (clear) and a blue mug on display at Royal Ontario Museum, Toronto.

BEADED ARCHED PANELS

See Beaded Arch.

BEADED BAND

Lee, "Early American Pressed Glass" Plate 61. Refers to it on pages 246-247. Giving nine forms that she had seen, stating that the syrup pitcher had a metal top, marked with the patent date, June 29, 84. Metz, Book two, pages 136-137 mentions it as having been made in colour. Canadian attribution by Sheeler, **"Burlington Glass Site" Canadian (antiques) Collector,** August, 1968.

BEADED FERN

Motif on mould-blown opal glass miniature lamp. See Stevens Canadian Glass 1825/1925. Page 219.

BEADED FLANGE

This pattern is listed as having been made in Ohio by the Fostoria Glass Company in 1891. Revi, **"American Pressed Glass and Figure Bottles,"** page 157. Not illustrated. Kamm-Wood **Book one,** page 83 shows the cream pitcher and states that forms known were four-piece table-set, pickle dish, sauce and flanged candlestick. It was said to have come in colour as well as crystal. Canadian attribution - Sheeler, **"Burlington Glass Site" Canadian (antiques) Collector,** June 1968. SCARCE.

BEADED GRAPE

Attributed to Burlington see Spence. **"Early Canadian Glass"** page 43. Also Sydenham Glass Co. Wallaceburg, Ontario. See small green glass dish on display Royal Ontario Museum, Toronto. Lee, **"Early American Pressed Glass",** pages 207/208 states "It was made over a period of years by the United States Glass Company of Pittsburgh, Pa." Originally called No. 15059 or **California Pattern.** Colours emerald green, clear glass. **Metz. Book One,** page 83 emphasizes "Flood of reproductions in both green and clear". **Kamm-Wood, book one** describes it as "Premium ware, given free with a pound of some Condiment". Revi, **"American Pressed Glass and Figure Bottles",** page 310, lists it as United States Glass Company, Ca. 1895. Page 321. He notes that Westmoreland Glass Company is producing this pattern in Milk Glass. It is said that the original pieces had gold trim and that this is not on reproduction items.

BEADED LATTICE AND FRAME

Opal mould-blown salt, number "10" on base. See Steven's Canadian Glass 1825/1925. Page 218.

BEADED OVAL AND FAN No. 1

Authenticated by Stevens, **Canadian Glass 1825-1925,** page 178. Spence, **Early Canadian Glass,** page 84. Jefferson Catalogue 21, No. 208 pattern.

BEADED OVAL AND FAN No. 2

Authenticated by Stevens, **Canadian Glass 1825-1925,** pages 171-172. Jeffersons Catalogue 21, No. 230 pattern. **Kamm-Wood, Book one,** page 18, lists this as **Arrow Head-In-Oval** stating origin of this pattern unknown.

BEADED OVAL AND SCROLL

A Bryce McKee pattern originally listed as **Dot.** It appears that the Burlington Glass Works produced many of the patterns which orginated with Bryce, McKee; Bryce, Higbee, and The J. B. Higbee companies. The same patterns were also produced in other Canadian factories. See Metz, book one pages 188-189.

BEADED OVAL WINDOW

Attributed to Burlington Glass Works. Shards found during "private digs" 1967. **Metz, Book One,** pages 158-159 gives no place of manufacture. **Kamm-Wood, Book Two,** lists this as **Oval Medallion.** Comes in clear, canary, amber, blue and a rare amethyst.

BLEEDING HEART

See Floral Ware.

BLOCK

Authenticated as a Canadian (Burlington) pattern by Stevens, **Canadian Glass 1825-1925,** page 214. Cream pitcher and sugar bowl on display at the Royal Ontario Museum, Toronto. Listed as **Clear Block, Metz, book one,** pages 164-165. **Kamm-Wood, book two,** page 58, shows the **Red Block.** This is the same pattern decorated with red on the blocks. By the amount to be found it is likely both versions were made in Canada. Block patterns have long been popular. **Red Block** known to be reproduced.

BLOCK BAND

Pitcher with Burlington mark.

BLOCK WITH FAN

See Stevens, **Early Canadian Glass,** page 67. Pickle inserts in both Acme and Toronto silver plate.

BOWTIE

See No. 204 pattern.

BOYD

Unknown Pattern listed on page 107, Stevens **Canadian Glass 1825-1925** under Goblets.

BUCKLE WITH DIAMOND BAND

Attributed to Burlington Glass Works. **Kamm-Wood, book one,** page 103 lists it as **Buckle and Diamond.** No maker indicated.

BULBOUS BULL'S EYE

Syrup Jug with **Burlington Mark.**

BULL'S EYE (Lamps)

Authenticated by Stevens, **Canadian Glass 1825-1925,** page 132. Dominion Glass Company Catalogue, No. 102 lamp. These lamps manufactured in flint and a wide variety of colors, also in opal. This pattern was used on shakers. Lamps on display at Royal Canadian Museum, Toronto.

BUTTERFLY WITH TASSEL

Authenticated by Stevens, **Canadian Glass 1825-1925,** page 217. Opal salt.

BUTTONS AND BOWS

See Nova Scotia Buttons and Bows.

BUTTON ARCHES

See **Metz Book Two,** pages 132-133. Dessert set in Toronto silver plate also Canadian souvenir mugs, opal tumblers and in custard.

CANADIAN

Authenticated by Stevens, **Canadian Glass 1825-1925,** page 212.

CANADIAN BEADED OVAL AND FAN No. 1
See Beaded Oval Fan No. 1

CANADIAN BEADED OVAL AND FAN No. 2
See Beaded Oval and Fan No. 2.

CANADIAN BLOCK
See Block.

CANADIAN DRAPE
Authenticated by Stevens, **Canadian Glass 1825-1925**, page 222. This pattern was used on lamps and tablewares. Lamp and Pitcher on display at Royal Ontario Museum. Pitcher has Burlington mark.

CANADIAN HEART
Attributed to Burlington Glass Works. Lamps come in Clear, Ivory, Custard, Blue, Turquoise and Green. Shards found of these colours and metal at Burlington site. The pattern was also used for shakers.

CANADIAN HORSESHOE
Authenticated by Stevens, **Canadian Glass 1825-1925.** Jefferson Glass Company Catalogue No. 21. **Pattern No. 221.** Known as **Ribbed Thumbprint.** See Revi, **American Pressed Glass,** page 206. Colours: Clear, Ivory, Custard ,also engraved and decorated with gold.

CANADIAN MAPLE LEAF
See Maple Leaf.

CANADIAN MOON AND STAR
Authenticated by Stevens, **Canadian Glass 1825-1925**, page 217. Seen on Shakers only to date. Opal, blue, white, pink and custard.

CANADIAN PILLAR
See Nova Scotia Crown.

CANADIAN PILLAR AND DIAMOND
See Nova Scotia Diamond Ray.

CANADIAN RAYED HEART
Authenticated by Stevens,**Canadian Glass 1825-1925,** page 127. Dominion Glass Catalogue lists this as No. 275 Ware. Clear and also seen in delicate green-blue with opal trim. SCARCE.

CANADIAN SHELL
Authenticated by Stevens, **Canadian Glass 1825-1925,** page 217. Opal lamps, delicate shading of colours. Shakers three colours also, pink to blue to white.

CANADIAN STIPPLED SWIRL AND STAR
Authenticated by Stevens, **Canadian Glass 1825-1925,** page 101. Catalogue Diamond Glass Works lists as **No. 200 Ware.** Design based on this pattern should not be confused, later pieces are less elaborate and the **Star** omitted. Some opal.

CANADIAN THISTLE
Also known as the **Jefferson No. 220 Set.** This was originally one of Higbee Glass Company designs and pieces from that factory have the Higbee trademark on them, that is a form of a "Bee" with the letters H.I.G. enclosed. Made in many forms and still a popular "collector" design. The Canadian made pieces differ, there is a thistle bud below the thistle flower and is not marked. See Stevens, **Canadian Glass 1825-1925,** pages 168-169.

CAPE COD
See Canadian

CENTENNIAL
See Nova Scotia Centennial

ETCHED GOBLETS

CHAIN

See Beaded Arch Panel

CHAIN WITH STAR

Attributed to Burlington Glass Works, Sheeler, **Burlington Glass Site, Canadian (antiques) Collector, June, 1968.** Metz, book one, 116-117. Lee, **Early American Pressed Glass,** 132. Complete table settings, wide variety of forms.

CHAMPAGNE

Unknown Pattern listed on page 107, Stevens, **Canadian Glass 1825-1925** under Goblets.

CHANDELIER

Spence, **Early Canadian Glass,** page 72, attributes this pattern to a Toronto Glass Works. Widely collected as a Canadian pattern. Very attractive, commands high prices. Lee, **Victorian Glass** refers to the pattern as **Crown Jewel.** Metz, **Book Two,** pages 130-131, uses the name **Chandelier,** also on pages 218-219 an inkwell is shown but has definite differences, the metal is not as brilliant or the pattern as well defined and the block band has no cross bars on block and the prisms are not as long. Revi, **American Pressed Glass,** page 275, lists it as a pattern of O'Hara Glass Company later re-issued by the United States Glass Company.

CHIPPENDALE

See Colonial.

CLEAR BLOCK

See Block.

COLONIAL

Authenticated by Stevens, **Canadian Glass 1825-1925,** pages 164-167 inclusive. Jefferson Catalogue No. 21, No. 1600 Set. Originally **Chippendale,** a design used by the Ohio Flint Glass Company who transferred the moulds together with their rights to the trade-mark "Krys-Tol" to Jefferson Glass Company in 1913. That year Jefferson acquired a Canadian factory buying the Independent Producers Co., Ltd. building in Toronto.

COLOSSUS

Attributed to Burlington Glass Works. Shards found "private digs" 1967. Metz, **Book One, pages** 176-177, does not mention place of manufacture. Kamm-Wood, **Book Two,** page 522, lists it as **Lacy Spiral.**

CONCORDIA

See Maple Leaf.

CORAL

See Fishscale.

CORINTHIAN

Attributed to Nova Scotia Glass Co.; c. 1886. See Spence, **Early Canadian Glass,** page 49. Not included in the MacLaren book **Nova Scotia Glass,** not mentioned in other glass books.

CORN

Authenticated by Stevens, **Canadian Glass 1825-1925,** page 217. Seen as Shakers only to date. Opal, white and blue. Likely to have been in pink and custard also.

Three variations of Deer and Dog Pattern goblet.

COSMOS

SUGAR

BUTTER DISH

CRUET

COSMOS

Attributed to Burlington Glass Works, similar shards found "private digs" 1967. Opaque white glass - dainty pattern. See Millard, **Opaque Glass,** plates 146-150, 191, 214 and 252. Kamm-Wood, **Book Two,** page 178. Says also known as **Stemless Daisy.** In "A Fifth Pitcher Book" Mrs. Kamm states "by whom or when the pattern was made or the original name have yet to be determined."

CROSS

Authenticated by Stevens, **Canadian Glass 1825-1925,** pages 214, 215, 222. Forms of this pattern on display at Royal Ontario Museum, Toronto. A comparison of the photographs and forms would indicate two different patterns. The first being that known as **Mikado Fan,** see Metz, **Book Two,** pages 148-149. The other **Boling,** see Millard, **Goblets, Two,** plate 138. Tableware being collected is of the **Mikado** pattern - goblet and lamps found in **Boling.**

CROWN JEWEL

See Chandelier.

CRYPTIC

See Nova Scotia Ribbon and Star.

DAHLIA

Attributed to Burlington Glass Works, shards found 'private digs' 1967. Lee, **American Pressed Glass,** pages 402-403. Plates 105, 126, 129, 130, 138. Colours, clear, blue, amber and yellow scarce.

ST. JOHN'S GOBLETS
QUEBEC

(FOSTER BROTHERS GLASS WORKS 1855 - 1875)

DAISY
Daisy without button. Pitcher. Burlington Handle.

DAISY AND BUTTON
Many variations of this design were produced at the Burlington Works. These wares were made in a variety of forms. Colours: light amber, dark amber, yellow, blue and clear. The dark amber seems the most collected. Blue is scarce. See Stevens, **Canadian Glass 1825-1925,** page 216 and include the following:

BELMONT DAISY
A pattern similar to **No. 100 Ware,** Belmont Glass Pattern 1886. But flat based. See Revi, **American Pressed Glass,** page 71. Burlington Marks on pitcher.

DAISY WITH CROSS BAR.
No. 99 Ware. Richards & Hartley. Also known as **Mikado** Ca. 1888.

DAISY WITH DEPRESSED BUTTON.
Queen. See **Kamm-Wood, Book Two,** page 477.

DAISY WITH PETTICOAT BAND
Kamm-Wood Book One, page 193 calls this **Daisy & Button Petticoat.** Place and date of manufacturer unknown.

DAISY WITH THUMBPRINT

DAISY WITH V ORNAMENT
Vandyke. See Revi, **American Pressed Glass,** pages 55, 59, 60, 151, 276, 315.

DAISY WITH X BAND
No. 240 Ware.

SQUARED DAISY AND DIAMOND
Authenticated by Burlington Mark on Water Pitcher handle. **Kamm-Wood, Book One,** page 186 remarks that the glass is fairly thick and heavy and that it has a ringing resonance.

DEWDROP WITH FLOWERS
See Nova Scotia Starflower.

DEWDROP WITH STAR
This motif shown on lamp bases made in Canada. See Stevens, **Canadian Glass 1825-1925,** page 220. This pattern was patented by Jenkins Jones of Campbell, Jones and Company, July 17th, 1877. The design was applied to a complete range of crystal tableware, plates in various styles and sizes also a patent dated lamp. Some of these pieces according to Revi are of transparent amber, blue and canary. See Revi, **American Pressed Glass,** page 98. Since other patterns made by this company were also produced at Burlington it could be that some Canadian made tableware will be found in the **Dewdrop with Star.**

DEER AND DOG
Attributed to Burlington Glass Works, see Sheeler, **'Burlington Glass Site', Canadian (antiques) Collector,** April 1968. A covered comport is on display at Royal Ontario Museum, Toronto. See, **Kamm-Wood, Book One,** page 195.

DERBY
See Pleat and Panel.

A bull's-eye in goblets

✳MRS. R. G. A., TORONTO

Congratulations! Your goblets permit the first published authentication of a recently documented form of nineteenth-century Canadian pressed glass. Last November I came across an early Canadian glass catalogue that named a number of nineteenth-century designs and among them I found documentation proving that the Canadian prototype of your goblets was produced circa 1885 under the original name, "Filly." It has been known for some time that several variants of the Filly design were produced in Canada. These have been titled in several ways: one of them, "Pointed Bull's-Eye." A close inspection of your Filly goblet shows that the upper and lower sections of the design containing the bull's-eye have been decorated with a notchlike embellishment.

The Filly goblet was produced circa 1885-1915 in several glass houses in Ontario and Quebec. According to my old catalogue, which was issued by the Diamond Glass Company, Montreal, the original cost of Filly goblets was forty-six dollars for "10

doz. Packed." The 1964 values ranged from $2.75 to $5 each, and 1965 will probably see the prices climb even higher.

The following list of books offers a basic bibliography for collectors interested in glass: *Glass*, by E. Barrington Haynes; *American Glass*, by George S. and Helen McKearin; *Collectors' Luck*, by F. St. George Spendlove; and *Early Canadian Glass*, by Gerald Stevens.

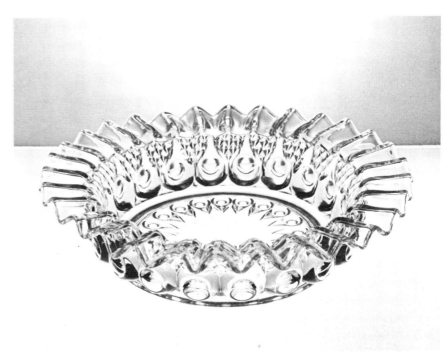

A Bull's-eye in Goblets.

1. & 2. *Photo copy of clipping - date unknown believed to be from a 1964* McLeans *Magazine.*
3. *FILLY goblet.*
4. *Spooner from pattern* SUNKEN BULL'S EYE *often called FILLY.*

5. *Shallow dish dia. 10" POINTED BULL'S EYE pattern.*

Note: This page should lessen the confusion and establish completely which pattern is FILLY.

DIAMOND

See Nova Scotia Diamond.

DIAMOND AND SUNBURST

See Lee, **American Pressed Glass**, pages 577-578. Pitchers found with **Burlington Mark.**

DIAMOND BAR

See Lattice.

DIAMOND MEDALLION

Attributed to the Diamond Glass Co. of Montreal. See Spence, **Early Canadian Glass,** page 95. Manufacturer unknown to American writers.

DIAMOND RAY

See Nova Scotia Diamond Ray.

DIAMOND WITH PEG

See Star.

DOG

See Deer and Dog.

DOG FINIAL

See Deer and Dog.

DOMINION

See Stevens, **Canadian Glass 1825-1925,** pages 99, 156 and 213. Similar pattern shown as **Minor Block,** Millard, **Goblets Two.** Metz, **Book One,** pages 150-151 refers to a like pattern as **Mascott. Domion** used on many forms including small to large candy jars.

EARLY JACOB'S LADDER

See Jacob's Ladder.

EARLY NUGGET

See Nugget.

ESTHER

Attributed Burlington Glass Works — **Burlington Mark.**

FEATHER BAND

See Spence, **Early Canadian Glass,** page 104, and **Stevens, Canadian Glass 1825-1925,** page 150. Kamm-Wood, **Book One,** shows this pattern as **Feather Band** on page 50. Glass brilliant and quite resonant. Complete range of table wares.

FEATHER DUSTER

Authenticated by Sheeler, **Burlington Glass Site, Canadian (antiques) Collector,** November 1968. Pattern used on table lamps, possibly table wares made in Canada. See Metz, **Book Two,** pages 174-175.

FLEUD-DE-LIS-AND SHELL

See Stevens, **Early Canadian Glass,** pages 64-65 design on opal covered sugar and creamer.

FILLY OR NOTCHED BULL'S EYE

Authenticated by Stevens, **Early Canadian Glass,** 62-63. **Canadian Glass 1825-1925,** page 52. Spence, **Early Canadian Glass,** page 42.

FINLAY

Not identified. Listed as 'Salts and Peppers'. Stevens, **Canadian Glass 1825-1925,** page 104.

MISCELLANEOUS

FEATHER DUSTER PATTERN FONTS

DEWDROP WITH STAR PATTERN FOOT

MUSTARD POT AND MUG VINE PATTERN

BURLINGTON FONT SMALL LAMP

CANADIAN HORSESHOE
FOOTED BUTTER DISH
FOOTED CREAM PITCHER

GREEK KEY HAND LAMP

FISHSCALE

Authenticated as Pressed Glass pattern used at Burlington Works. See Stevens, **Canadian Attic**, page 130. Lamp displayed at the Royal Ontario Museum. **Coral** - American tableware known as <u>Fishscale</u>.

FLORAL

See Nova Scotia Floral.

FLORAL WARE

Also known as **Bleeding Heart**. King Glass Company pattern. Attributed Burlington Glass Works. See Stevens, **Canadian Glass 1825-1925**, page 106.

FLOWER AND QUILL

Attributed to Burlington Glass Works. Shards found in "private digs" 1967. Metz, **Book Two**, 54-55, refers to it as previously called **Pretty Band**, but lists it as **Flower and Quill**. Kamm-Wood, **Book One**, page 254, remarks on the resemblance of this pattern to **Picket** and **Panelled Thousand Eye**. Colours: clear, delicate green and pale yellow, could also be blue.

FORGET-ME-NOT

See Stevens, **Canadian Glass 1825-1925**, page 219. Opal glass shakers. (Bottle shaped.)

FRAME AND SHELL

See Stevens, **Canadian Glass 1825-1925**, page 218. Opal glass shakers. No. 8 design.

FRAME AND SPRIG

See Stevens, **Canadian Glass 1825-1925**, page 222. Lamps found in a variety of sizes.

FROSTED FLOWER BAND

Attributed to Burlington Glass Works. Lee, **American Pressed Glass** plates 107, 109, pages 576-577, lists it under **Flower Band**. Origin and maker not known.

FROSTED BUTTERFLY

A lamp with this design plus the anchor-in-horseshoe (seen on the **Good Luck pattern**) authenticated as Burlington by Sheeler, Burlington Glass Site, **Canadian (antiques) Collector**, July 1968.

FISHSCALE LAMPS

1. *Honeycomb Lamp and Goblet.*

2. *Goblet ht. 8", dia 4½".*

3. *Grape and Festoon with Shield Goblet Variants.*

4. *Beaded Oval and Fan. No. 2 Bowl on Stem (rare).*

GALAXY

See Nova Scotia Gothic.

GALLOWAY

See Woodrow.

GARDEN OF EDEN

See Lotus.

GARFIELD DRAPE

See Canadian Drape.

GESNER

The name given to Lamp authenticated as being produced at Burlington Glass Works, see Sheeler, **Burlington Glass Site, Canadian (antiques) Collector,** July 1968. Lamp displayed at Royal Ontario Museum, Toronto. So named to honor Dr. Abraham Gesner, a Nova Scotia physician and geologist who revolutionized lighting with the discovery of kerosene. See Russell, **"Heritage of Light"**, pages 130-151, inclusive.

GOOD LUCK ?

Truly a question mark pattern. Being collected for several reasons. It closely resembles **Tassel and Crest.** The Anchor and Horseshoe motif is part of an authenticated Canadian pattern. See Sheeler, Burlington Glass Site, **Canadian (antiques) Collector,** July, 1968. An Oddfellow Goblet with the Oddfellow Insignia instead of the **Prayer Mat** is identical in other respects to the **Good Luck** goblet. The Nova Scotia Glass Company in 1887 curtailed the manufacturing of lamp chimneys to make more pressed glass and tumblers engraved with Masonic and Oddfellow emblems, see MacLaren, **Nova Scotia Glass,** page 14.

GRADUATED DIAMOND

Goblet only. Attributed to Burlington Glass works, see Sheeler, Burlington Glass Site, **Canadian (antiques) Collector,** May 1968.

GRAPE AND FESTOON

Attributed to Burlington Glass Works.

GRAPE AND FESTOON WITH SHIELD

Shards found at Burlington Glass site, goblet on display at Royal Ontario Museum. Revi, **American Pressed Glass,** page 138, shows covered comport and says "possibly produced by Doyle and Company, Pittsburgh". This company was established in Pittsburgh, Penn. in 1866, absorbed into the United States Glass Company by 1891. Flint, blue, amber and green.

GRAPE AND VINE

See Nova Scotia Grape and Vine.

GREEK KEY AND WEDDING RING

See Stevens, **Early Canadian Glass,** pages 62, 63 and 67. Opalescent blue, opalescent white. Complete range of tablewares made. Burlington Glass.

GREEK LYRE AND DART

Design on small opal tray, see Stevens, **Canadian Glass 1825-1925,** page 219, base designs include a rayed circle and sawtooth motif. Burlington glass.

HOBNAIL

See Nova Scotia Hobnail.

HONEYCOMB

Listed by the Diamond Glass Co., Ltd., as **New York.** See Stevens, **Canadian Glass 1825-1925,** pages 105 ,107, 109, also Metz, **Book Two,** pages 44-45. **Honeycomb with Diamond.** This version of the pattern is most frequently found in Canadian stores.

1. Honeycomb Etched Goblets.

2. Pillow Encircled Celery Vase.

3. Chandelier. Cream Pitcher.

4. Chandelier. Cream Pitcher Variant.

5. Sawtooth Miniature Sugar and Cream Pitcher

6. Sawtooth. Nappy Dia. 4"

HONEYCOMB WITH DIAMOND
See Honeycomb.

HORSESHOE
See Canadian Horseshoe.

IDA
See Sheraton.

IMPERIAL
Listed as comport on page 105 Stevens, **Canadian Glass 1825-1925.** See Jacob's ladder.

INDIANA
See Stevens, **Canadian Glass 1825-1925. Indiana** listed as goblet. See Kamm-Wood, **Book Two,** page 340, also, Lee, **Victorian Glass,** page 39. This is a pattern made by United States Glass Company 1898. Several of the patterns now known to have been manufactured by companies later absorbed by U.S. Glass Co. were also made in Canadian factories.

INTERLOCKING LOOP
Jefferson No. 2 Ware, sometimes called **The Jefferson,** also known as their No. 254 pattern. See Revi, **American Pressed Glass,** page 208. Colors: rose and gold.

IVORINA VERDE
Advertised in 1915 Jefferson Catalogue in two forms. **Hair Receiver** and a **Puff Box.** Not known if Jefferson made it in any other forms. This is a Heisey Company pattern c. 1899. Opaque ivory colored glass with green trim. See Kamm-Wood, **Book Two,** page 335.

IRIS WITH MEANDER
Jefferson pattern, believed to have been made in Canada after 1912. Advertised by them as "Iris" better known by the former name. See Kamm-Wood, **Book Two,** page 355. The pattern is similar to the **No. 270** ware shown on page 191, Stevens, **Canadian Glass 1825-1925.** The difference lies in the irregular band of Iris around the base of the body connected by thin meandering lines. Base of this pattern ornamented by large 24 rayed star. Also listed as **Jefferson 1** pattern, Kamm-Wood, **Book Two,** page 348. Plain, coloured and opal.

JACOB'S LADDER
Attributed to Burlington Glass Works, shards found "private digs". The pattern was patented by John Bryce on June 13th, 1876 as **Imperial.** This pattern was listed under comports on page 105, Stevens, **Canadian Glass 1825-1925.** Full range of tablewares made. Clear and Amber. Finials, Maltese Cross. The pattern was also advertised as **Maltese.** There are two types of **Jacob's Ladder,** early and late. **Late Jacob's Ladder** is heavier and not as attractive as **Early Jacob's Ladder.** See Lee, **American Pressed Glass,** plates 50 and 57 also Kamm-Wood, **Book Two,** page 346.

JEWEL AND SHELL
See Nugget.

KELLER
Not identified, see Stevens, **Canadian Glass 1825-1925.** Listed as goblet, page 107.

KENLEE
See Nova Scotia Kenlee.

KEY AND RING
See Greek Greek Key and Wedding Ring.

KRYSTOL
See Star.

LACY SPIRAL
See Collosus.

WHIMSEYS

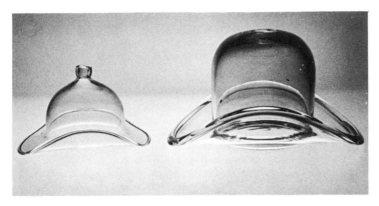

Hats in Nova Scotia Museum.

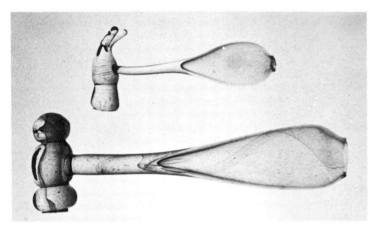

Two hammers in Nova Scotia Museum.

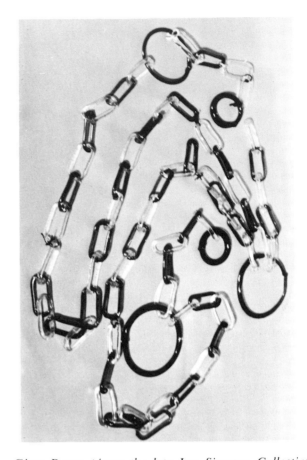

Glass Drape (from the late Lee Simpson Collection).

Odd piece, could be start of **hammer**.

Pear.

Swan (Wallaceburg)

Flying Bird.

LATTICE

Attributed to Burlington Glass Works. Shards found "private digs" 1967. See Kamm-Wood **Book Two**, page 360. Mrs. Kamm had previously referred to this pattern as **"Diamond Bar"**. She says the creamer resembles that of many others in shape — **Scalloped Tape**, **Parthenon (Egyptian)**, **Minerva** and **Good Luck**. See Revi, **American Pressed Glass**, page 217. **King's No. 20 Ware**. Stevens, **Canadian Glass 1825-1925** lists No. 20 as unidentified pattern. See page 100.

LEAF AND DART

Authenticated by Sheeler, **Burlington Glass Site**, Canadian (antiques) **Collector**. August 1968. See Lee, **Early American Pressed Glass**, page 307, plate 95. Goblet on display at Royal Ontario Museum, Toronto. Pattern resembles **Arabesque**.

LILY-OF-THE-VALLEY

Attributed to Burlington Glass Works, shards found "private digs" 1967. See Kamm-Wood **Book Two**, page 373. "Chipman says it is definitely "Sandwich". Mrs. Kamm stated that she failed to find any broken bits of it at the Massachusetts Institute of Technology and this absence has little meaning for not all the Sandwich patterns could be expected to be represented by the accidental find of a quantity of broken glass under a pavement at the site of an old factory. It was her opinion that circumstantial evidence placed the pattern as Sandwich since it so closely resembled known Sandwich patterns.

LILY-OF-THE-VALLEY-ON-LEGS

The second form of this pattern has three legs. Likely a later version. See Kamm-Wood, **Book Two**, page 373. The **Lily of the Valley** was a popular motif on pitcher and tumbler sets, enamelled on glass. Colours — pale green, blue, light amber and cranberry.

LION

Attributed to Burlington Glass Works. Water pitchers found with Burlington Mark.

LOOP AND PILLAR

A pattern found as inserts in Toronto and Acme Silver Plate especially Bride's baskets. Kamm-Wood, **Book One**, page 104 named it **Panelled Jewel**. (There is another pattern of that name). She later made reference to this pattern as **Michigan** and stated that it was the original name. This is a U.S. Glass Co. pattern produced after 1893. The authors have found it quite plentiful in Canadian stores and at the shows. Some with ruby and gilt trim, mostly clear, a few pieces have been seen in an attractive blue. See Kamm-Wood, **Book Two**, page 401. It has long been a favorite with American visitors to Canada under the name of **Michigan**. The name we list it under is that given by Metz, **Book One**, pages 194-195.

LYRE AND DART

See Greek Lyre and Dart.

MAPLE LEAF

One of the favorite patterns of the Canadian glass collector, produced by many factories including Burlington Glass Works, Ontario (1875-1909); Diamond (1892-1903); Diamond Flint (1904-1913) and Dominion Glass (1913-   ) Companies of Ontario and Quebec. The Jefferson (Canadian) Glass Company Limited show the Maple Leaf as **No. 205** Ware or Set. See page 177, Stevens, **Can-**

MARQUIS of LORNE

Marquis & Marchioness of Lorne landed in Halifax N.S. 25th November - 1878. A commemorative ware, — also in colours — Opal, White, Purple, Slag, Blue, Amber, etc.

adian Glass 1825-1925. The pattern was produced in clear, coloured and opaque, white and opal blue glass tablewares. There are three styles of Canadian Maple Leaf. See Spence, **Early Canadian Glass,** pages 64, 73, 74, 75, 76, 77, 78, 79, 80 and 88. **Concordia** being a name for the variant of the leaf as shown on the Montreal "Concordia Plate". The other types would seem to be typical of Ontario made pieces.

MARQUIS OF LORNE

Although this pattern has been attributed to many Canadian glass works by Stevens, see **Early Canadian Glass ,**page XIII of the introduction. The authors have been unable to find a form of this design which does not have the trade-mark of the English Manufacturer. This trade-mark is very tiny and often hard to find. We have examined some thirty to forty items including five four piece sets, these were in clear, coloured and opal glass. However this pattern should be considered part of any Canadian glass collection since it was made to commemorate an historical Canadian event.

MARY GARDINER TYPE

Authenticated by Stevens, **Early Canadian Glass,** pages 51-52. Listed with special pieces. **Burlington.** The original specimen was made by Mr. Roth, circa 1882. The Mary Gardiner pitcher was a present to the mother of George Gardiner from Mr. Roth, who was a highly expert glass-maker. This is shown by the variety of techniques used in the making of the pitcher. It is quite possible that the **Burlington Mark** dates from around this time as pitchers of the **Mary Gardiner Type** have been found so marked.

MINERVA

Attributed to Burlington Glass Works. Shards found "private digs" 1967. Kamm-Wood, **Book Two,** page 402. Metz, **Book One,** pages 108-109 attributes this pattern to the Sandwich factory. Not mentioned by Revi, **American Pressed Glass.** Good selection of tablewares on shelves in Canadian stores.

NOTCHED BULL'S EYE

Better known as **Filly.** A Bull's eye varient authenticated by Stevens **Canadian Glass 1825-1925,** page 107. There seems to be some confusion with regard to these bull's eye variants. The authors have found that **Filly, Sunken** and **Pointed Bull's Eye** are three definite variations and not to be mistaken for each other. See Spence, **Early Canadian Glass,** pages 42 and 72.

NOVA SCOTIA ACADIAN

See MacLaren, **Nova Scotia Glass,** page 16.

NOVA SCOTIA BUTTONS AND BOWS

See Millard, **Goblets, Book Two,** page 147. Metz, **Book Two,** pages 200-201. Mrs. Metz mentions "only goblet" has been found. See MacLaren, **Nova Scotia Glass,** page 33.

NOVA SCOTIA CENTENNIAL

This pattern was named in honor of Canada's Centennial, 1967. See MacLaren, **Nova Scotia Glass,** page 31. Spence, **Early Canadian Glass,** page 71, suggests the name **Bars and Squares.**

NOVA SCOTIA CROWN

Better known to collectors as **Pillar.** Metz, **Book One,** pages 196-197. Pattern McKee's catalogue of 1894. Cruet listed in their 1917 catalogue. Finial Maltese Cross. Kamm-Wood, **Book Two,** refers to it as **Ball.** Also known as **Notched Bar** Metz, **Book Two,** pages 196 - 197. See MacLaren, **Nova Scotia Glass,** page 27. Syrup Jug seen with Burlington Mark.

MISCELLANEOUS

THREE EGG CUPS

N.S. DIAMOND BIRD FEEDER

JACOB'S LADDER MASTER SALT

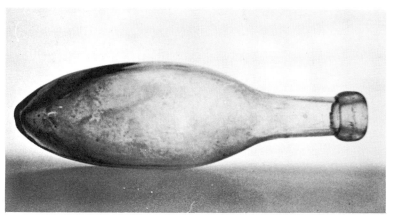

UNUSUAL BOTTLE

N.S. DIAMOND INKWELL

N.S. DIAMOND DRESSER JAR

VICTORIA COMMEMORATIV
JIGGER

NOVA SCOTIA DIAMOND

This pattern was also a product of Ontario factories. See Stevens, **Canadian Glass 1825-1925**, page 215. Spence, **Early Canadian Glass**, page 72 and MacLaren, **Nova Scotia Glass**, page 27. Popular in full range of tablewares, toilet articles, pin boxes, etc.

NOVA SCOTIA DIAMOND RAY

This pattern has been known by several names. Authenticated as a Nova Scotia pattern. **Diamond Ray seems an apt description.** Stevens, **Canadian Glass 1825-1925**, page 64, refers to it as **Pillar and Diamond**. Spence, **Early Canadian Glass**, pages 62 and 69, calls it **Prism and Diamond** and Metz, **Book One**, pages 198-199 **Bar and Fine Cut**. See MacLaren, **Nova Scotia Glass**, page 28.

NOVA SCOTIA FLORAL

See MacLaren, **Nova Scotia Glass**, page 27. Metz, **Book Two**, pages 66-67 refers to the pattern as **Round Marsh Pink** and lists it as a scarce member of the Marsh Pink family. **Square Marsh Pink** is a variant of this pattern.

NOVA SCOTIA GOTHIC

Whilst this pattern has been mentioned by Stevens, **Canadian Glass 1825-1925**, page 61 and Spence, **Early Canadian Glass**, page 61, as well as authenticated in MacLaren, **Nova Scotia Glass**, page 27. It is known only as a goblet. The authors have not found it any other form. Metz, **Book Two,** listing it under the name of **Galaxy,** see pages 150-151 does not state only goblet.

NOVA SCOTIA GRAPE AND VINE

A pattern which is most collectable, and is in fact found in a variety of forms and in many parts of Canada, getting scarcer as demand increases for this very Canadian design. Authenticated by MacLaren **Nova Scotia Glass**, pages 19-20. See Stevens, **Early Canadian Glass**, page 143. Spence, **Early Canadian Glass**, pages 47, 48 and 62. Metz, **Book Two**, pages 198-199 lists it as a Canadian pattern but refers to it as **Ramsay Grape.**

NOVA SCOTIA HOBNAIL

The two pieces seen would appear to be part of the **Crown** pattern.

NOVA SCOTIA KENLEE

Authenticated by **MacLaren, Nova Scotia Glass**, page 18. Stevens, **Canadian Glass 1825-1925**, page 61. Spence, **Early Canadian Glass**, page 60. In Metz, **Book One**, pages 126-127 it is listed as **Ribbon Band with Pendants**. So far only goblet known, perhaps like other patterns, once known and searched for different forms will be found.

NOVA SCOTIA QUEEN VICTORIA COMMEMORATIVE 1837-1897.

Highly treasured by collectors, families who own these pieces do not part with them readily, this pattern is part of Canadian history. Made in four piece set, four forms of bread plate, nappies, pitchers and a most attractive covered bowl. There are variations of the pattern. Some pieces have rayed bases, others waffled and yet another has medallion and cross base. The finials are the same on all covered pieces. Seen with single or double head designs some with medallion or ray the others with wreath. Canadian authentication MacLaren, **Nova Scotia Glass**, page 31. Spence, **Early Canadian Glass**, pages 28 and 64. Stevens, **Early Canadian Glass**, pages 144-145.

NOVA SCOTIA RASPBERRY

The Raspberry motif is simple but attractive. As with other Nova Scotia patterns there seems to be a plain and a fancy set of ware.

NAPPIES

NOVA SCOTIA CROWN

SHERATON

LEAF AND DART

LILY OF THE VALLEY

DAHLIA

PANELLED FORGET-ME-NOT

CANADIAN - CAPE COD

NOVA SCOTIA NAPPY

Ribbed Band was plain and **Grape and Vine** fancy, yet both were basically the same ware. So it is with Raspberry and the following pattern **Raspberry and Shield**. Both patterns are shown by MacLaren, **Nova Scotia Glass**, pages 15-17. Spence, **Early Canadian Glass**, pages 52 and 61. Stevens, **Canadian Glass 1825-1925**, page 61 shows **Raspberry**. Both of these patterns also made at Burlington Works.

NOVA SCOTIA RASPBERRY AND SHIELD

See Nova Scotia Raspberry.

NOVA SCOTIA RIBBED BAND

Another pattern that has changed names. Stevens, **Early Canadian Glass**, pages 142 and 157 **Fine Rib**. Spence, **Early Canadian Glass**, page 62, **Ribbed**. Metz, **Book Two**, pages 198-199, **Pleated Bands** and Kamm-Wood, **Book Two**, page 456 lists it as **Petticoat Fluting**. Canadian authentication MacLaren, **Nova Scotia Glass**, pages 27-30.

NOVA SCOTIA RIBBON AND STAR

Also known as **Zippered Block No. 15** manufactured by George A. Duncan & Sons, Penn. See Revi, **American Pressed Glass**, page 149. Metz, **Book Two**, page 162 names it **Open Cryptic**. Authenticated as Canadian, MacLaren, **Nova Scotia Glass**, page 12.

NOVA SCOTIA STARFLOWER

This pattern seems to have several variations, possibly this could depend on where it was made. It is known that it was produced not only in Nova Scotia but also in New Brunswick and Quebec. George MacLaren shows two very distinct variations. The Starflower in his **Nova Scotia Glass**, 1965, sugar bowl on page 15 is different to the flowers depicted on the comport and water pitcher same page. Spence, **Early Canadian Glass**, pages 44, 45, 46, 62, 64, 68 and 88 show variations, one of which they attribute to New Brunswick. Metz, **Book Two**, pages 198-199 lists the pattern as **Dewdrops With Flowers** also **Quantico**.

NOVA SCOTIA TANDEM

Previously known as **Tandem Bicycle**. See Metz, **Book Two**, pages 132-133. This pattern seems scarce even in Nova Scotia. Shown on page 8 MacLaren, **Nova Scotia Glass**. Stevens, **Canadian Glass 1825-1925** page 61. Spence, **Early Canadian Glass**, pages 60-61.

NOVA SCOTIA TASSEL AND CREST

The most fascinating of Nova Scotia glass. The pattern includes so many motifs — crossed trumpets forming a crest, a shield, palm trees with star overhead, stretched wings, scalloped band with pendants between what could be bells, three feathers for the finial and a rayed base. As if that were not enough the handle of the pieces are quite ornate. Complete sets of tableware have been found but is there a goblet? Perhaps a study of historical events connected with Victoria would reveal what inspired the designer. Metz, **Book Two**, pages 198-199 calls it **Pins and Bells**. Canadian authentication, MacLaren, **Nova Scotia Glass**, page 28. Also shown in Stevens, **Early Canadian Glass**, page 153. Spence, **Early Canadian Glass**, pages 51 and 53.

NUGGET

Which had been previously made at the Sydenham Glass Company factory in Wallaceburg was also made by Jefferson's. The Nugget produced in Toronto was a variant on the Sydenham pattern and became known to the collectors as **Late Nugget**. Sydenham Glass Company was also part of the Dominion Glass Company. Known as **Shell and Jewel** see Kamm-Wood **Book Two**, pages 198-199. Clear and coloured.

TUMBLERS

LAKEFIELD CUT GLASS

BEADED GRAPE

POINTED BULL'S EYE

ATHENIAN

FEATHER BAND

TOTEM

Note - Tumblers are scarce

48

NUMBERED PATTERNS

No.   **1 JEFFERSON** see Iris With Meander.

No.   **2 JEFFERSON** see Interlocking Loop.

No.   **11 ADAMS** see Thousand Eye.

No.   **15 GEORGE DUNCAN** see Honeycomb.

No.   **19 FINDLAY** see Findlay 19. Kamm-Wood **Book One,** page 250.

No.   **20 KING** see Lattice.

No.   **24 BRYCE, McKEE** see Panelled Forget-Me-Not.

No.   **79 BRYCE, McKEE** see Chain With Star.

No.   **82 O'HARA** see Chandelier.

No.   **99 RICHARDS & HARTLEY** see Daisy and Button Cross Bar.

No. **100 BELMONT see** Daisy and Button, Belmont Daisy.

No. **101 DOMINION** see No. 101 Lamp. Stevens, **Canadian Glass 1825-1925,** page 126.

No. **101 BURLINGTON** see Stevens, **Canadian Glass, 1825-1925,** page 223.

No. **102 DOMINION** see Bull's Eye. Lamps and shakers.

No. **105 DOMINION** see Bead and Petal. Lamps and tablewares.

No. **106 DOMINION** One Piece Lamp. See Stevens, **Canadian Glass 1825-1925,** page 130.

No. **128 BRYCE,McKEE** see Cross.

No. **198 KING** see Vine. Mug.

No. **200 JEFFERSON see** Stipple Swirl and Star.

No. **204 JEFFERSON** Authenticated by Stevens, **Canadian Glass 1825-1925.** Jefferson Catalogue 21. No. 204 Pattern. Has been named **Bowtie.** Not to be confused with another pattern of the same name. Metz, **Book Two,** pages 116-117. **Millard, Goblets Two,** plate 5. There are definite differences. The Jefferson pattern being composed of curved crossed lines from base to top and forming a diamond border. The indentations across the centre section of the pattern may be the reason for misnomer. Suggest **No. 204** pattern be used until a better name found.

No. **205 JEFFERSON** see Maple Leaf.

No. **206 DIAMOND** see New Century. Not identified.

No. **207 DIAMOND** A quality ware. See Stevens, **Canadian Glass 1825-1925,** page 106. Nappies. note price $4.80.

No. **208 JEFFERSON** see Beaded Oval and Fan No. 1.

No. **210 JEFFERSON** see Bead and Petal.

No. **211 JEFFERSON** see Shell.

No. **212 JEFFERSON** see Tokyo.

No. **220 JEFFERSON** see Canadian Thistle.

No. **221 JEFFERSON** see Canadian Horseshoe.

No. **230 JEFFERSON** see Beaded Oval and Fan No. 2.

No. **240 JEFFERSON** see Daisy and X Band.

No. **250 JEFFERSON** see Ribbed Drape.

No. **251 JEFFERSON** Not named, see Revi, **American Pressed Glass,** page 208.

No. **254 JEFFERSON** see No. 2.

No. **270 JEFFERSON** Not named. See Stevens, **Canadian Glass 1825-1925,** pages 191-192.

No. **271 JEFFERSON** Not named. See Revi, **America Pressed Glass,** page 209.

No. **275 JEFFERSON** see Rayed Heart.

Pipes were popular souvenir items and came in a variety of colours.

RUBY FLASH

CANADIAN

NS GANONG CANDY MUG

BUTTON ARCHES

SOUVENIR *of* SASKATOON

CANADIAN HORSESHOE

No. 307 RIVERSIDE see Marsh Fern. Burlington Mark Pitcher.

No. 358 JEFFERSON Not named. See Stevens, **Canadian Glass 1825-1925,** pages 184, 185 and 186.

No. 353 JEFFERSON Not named. See Stevens, **Canadian Glass 1825-1925,** page 187.

No. 279 JEFFERSON Not named. See Stevens, **Canadian Glass 1825-1925,** page 193.

No. 555 GEORGE DUNCAN see Shell and Tassel. Insert in Toronto Plate.

No. 603 FOSTORIA see Robin Hood. Burlington Mark Syrup Jug.

No. 1600 JEFFERSON see Colonial.

No. 1883 JEFFERSON see page 180 Stevens, **Canadian Glass, 1825-1925,** clear and coloured glass.

No. 15029 U.S.GLASS COMPANY see Indiana. Catalogue Diamond Glass Co. See Stevens, **Canadian Glass 1825-1925,** page 107.

OAK LEAF AND INVERTED FLEUR DE LIS

Motif on mould blown opal shakers, see Stevens, **Canadian Glass 1825-1925,** page 218.

OLD OAKEN BUCKET

See Stevens, **Canadian Glass 1825-1925,** page 111. **Kamm-Wood, Book Two,** page 623. Metz, **Book One,** pages 128-129. Jelly container had "**The Old Oaken Bucket**" stamped on the metal lid. Made in clear, amber, canary, blue, amethyst, opal, white and blue. Bryce McKee pattern, Ca. 1880.

PALMETTE

Authenticated by Stevens, **Canadian Glass 1825-1925, page 214.** Not attributed to any factory by American writers. Burlington.

PANELLED FORGET-ME-NOT

Authenticated by Stevens, **Canadian Glass 1825-1925,** page 216. No. 24, Bryce,McKee, Ca. 1875. Also known as **Regal.** Doyle & Co. pattern.

PANELLED THISTLE

See **Canadian Thistle.**

PANELLED THOUSAND EYE

Two and three panel attributed Burlington Glass Works. Not yet authenticated.

PERT

See **Ribbed Forget-Me-Not.**

PICKET

Attributed to Burlington Glass Works. Shards found 1967 "private digs". Metz, **Book One,** pages 131-132. King Glass Company pattern. Also known as **London.**

PILLOW ENCIRCLED

Water Pitcher seen with **Burlington Mark.**

PIONEER

See **Westward Ho.**

PLEAT AND PANEL

Attributed to Burlington Glass Works. Sheeler, **Burlington Glass Site, Canadian (antiques) Collector.** April 1968. Bryce, McKee Co. pattern Ca. 1882. Also known as **Derby.**

POINTED BULL'S EYE

Attributed to Canadian Glass Factories. See Stevens, **Early Canadian Glass,** page 163 and Metz, **Book Two,** page 199. Also known as **Reverse Torpedo.**

WINE GLASSES

CHAIN & STAR

DAISY & DEPRESSED BUTTON

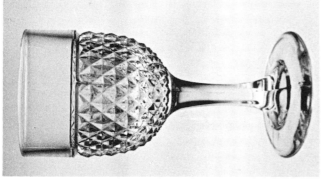

NOVA SCOTIA DIAMOND

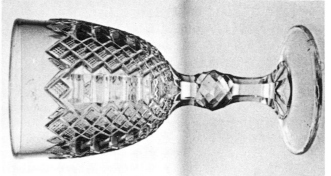

JACOB'S LADDER

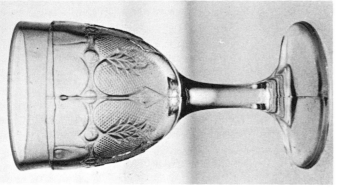

LEAF & DART

DIAMOND MEDALLION

NOVA SCOTIA TANDEM

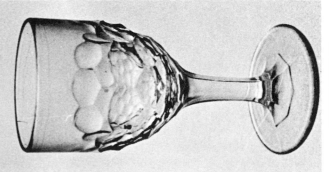

HONEYCOMB

52

PRINCESS FEATHER

Variant of this pattern used on salt shakers and table lamps. Clear and coloured, opal. Burlington. See Stevens, **Early Canadian Glass,** pages 66 and 69.

QUEEN

See **Daisy** and **Depressed Button.**

RAMSAY GRAPE

See **Nova Scotia Grape and Vine.**

RASPBERRY

See **Nova Scotia Raspberry.**

RASPBERRY AND SHIELD

See **Nova Scotia Raspberry and Shield.**

RAYED HEART

See **Canadian Rayed Heart.**

REGAL

See **Panelled Forget-Me-Not.**

RIBBED BAND

See **Nova Scotia Ribbed Band.**

RIBBED FORGET-ME-NOT

Attributed to Burlington Glass Works. See Sheeler, Burlington Glass Site, **Canadian (antiques) Collector,** January 1969. Bryce, McKee Pattern Ca. 1880. **Pert.**

RIBBED DRAPE

Jefferson No. 250 Ware, made in clear, opaque ivory and opaque blue glass all with gold trim.

RIBBED THUMBPRINT

See **Canadian Horseshoe.**

RIBBON AND STAR

See **Nova Scotia Ribbon and Star.**

ROBIN HOOD

Attributed to Burlington. Syrup jug with **Burlington Mark.** Fostoria No. 603. See Kamm-Wood, **Book One,** page 492.

SAWTOOTH

Attributed to Burlington Glass Works. See Sheeler, Burlington Glass Site, **Canadian (antiques) Collector,** August 1968. A pattern made by several American factories including Bryce, McKee. Also known as **Diamond.**

SHELL AND TASSEL

Seen in Canadian silver plate. Some forms resemble **Tassel and Crest** dishes.

SHERATON

Attributed to Burlington Glass Works. Shards found ''private digs'' 1967. A Bryce, Higbee and Company pattern. Ca. 1885. Also known as **Ida.**

SCRAMBLED WHEELS

See **Totem.**

SNAIL

Attributed to Burlington. Syrup Jug with **Burlington Mark.** A George Duncan Pattern. Ca. 1885.

SQUARED DAISY AND DIAMOND

Attributed to Burlington Glass Works. Shards found ''private digs'' 1967. Very like **Argyle.** A Campbell Jones & Co. pattern. Ca. 1890.

SQUARE MARSH PINK

A pattern similar to **Nova Scotia Floral.** Attributed to Burlington Glass Works. Shards found ''private digs'' 1967. Found in clear and amber glass.

SUNKEN BULL'S EYE

BEADED GRAPE

BEADED OVAL AND FAN
No. 2

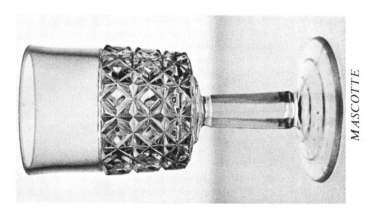

MASCOTTE

DAISY AND X BAND

FILLY

CANADIAN

BLOCK BAND

STAR

Jefferson Pattern. Trademark **"Krystol"**.

STARFLOWER

See Nova Scotia Starflower.

STIPPLED SWIRL AND STAR

Authenticated by Stevens, **Canadian Glass 1825-1925,** page 101. Catalogue of Diamond Glass Co., Montreal. Jefferson No. 200 Ware Made also in opal.

SUNKEN BULL'S EYE

See **Notched Bull's Eye.**

SWIRL

Opal salt shaker shown on page 217 Stevens, **Canadian Glass 1825-1925.** Also seen as syrup jug.

TANDEM BICYCLE

See **Nova Scotia Tandem.**

TASSEL AND CREST

See **Nova Scotia Tassel and Crest.**

THE JEFFERSON

See **Interlocking Loop.**

THOUSAND EYE

Attributed to Burlington Glass Works. Shards found "private digs" 1967. Adams & Company No. 11 pattern. Ca. 1874. Clear and amber.

TOTEM

Attributed to Toronto or Wallaceburg by Spence, **Early Canadian Glass,** page 85. Syrup found with **Burlington Mark.** Metz refers to this pattern as **Scrambled Wheels,** see **Book Two,** pages 204-205. A child's mug is shown and I quote "it belongs to no other pattern". Cream pitcher found with **Burlington Mark.**

TRAILWORK

Attributed to Nova Scotia or Quebec. See Spence, **Early Canadian Glass,** pages 66-67. Colours: clear, blue, green.

TREE OF LIFE

Seen in Canadian silver plate, also Water Pitcher with **Burlington Mark.** Colours: clear, blue, amber.

VICTORIA COMMEMORATIVE

See Nova Scotia Queen Victoria Commemorative.

VINE

King No. 198 pattern. Shards found Burlington Glass Works, "private digs" 1967. Small mug. See Revi, **American Pressed Glass,** page 217.

VIRGINIA

See Woodrow.

WESTWARD HO

Attributed to Burlington Glass Works. See Sheeler, Burlington Glass Site, **Canadian (antiques) Collector,** August 1968. A Gillinder and Sons pattern. Also known as **Pioneer.** Metz, **Book One,** pages 110-111 refers to it as having been reproduced in most forms.

WOODROW

Gerald Stevens renamed the popular pattern **Galloway** and called it "Woodrow" as a tribute to Mrs. Woodrow of Ontario. See Stevens, **Canadian Glass 1825-1925,** page 180. Known as **Galloway.** Also called **Virginia.** See Metz, **Book One,** pages 218-219.

ZIPPERED BLOCK

See Nova Scotia Ribbon and Star.

AEGIS

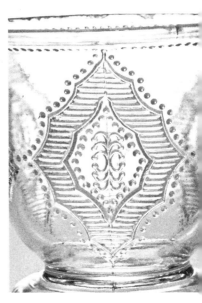

AEGIS

1. *Four Piece Set*
   Creamer, Butter dish, Suga
   (lid missing), Spoon.
2. *Pickle Dish. ht. 1½", wd. 5.*
   Long. 7".
3. *Open butter.*
4. *Aegis Motif.*

Note the changing shape of pat
tern motifs from form to form
Aegis is a good example — on on
piece it appears diamond shaped
on another triangle, on tall piece
it is almost oval, the number o
scroll lines also varies within th
motif.

ANDERSON

ANDERSON

1. Covered comport. ht. 10½", dia. 8"
   Cream ht. 5"
   Nappy ht. 2", dia. 3¾"

2. Covered Sugar

3. Nappy dia. 7".

ATHENIAN

ATHENIAN

1. 4 piece set (Creamer should have cover.)
   Covered Sugar, Butter dish, Spoon.
2. Water Pitcher half gallon.
3. Cake Stand Dia. 9".
4. Open Comport (note foot) dia. 8".
   (Note. Made in full range of table wares — nappy
   dia. 4" nappy dia. 8". Shakers — and individual butter pots. Colours — clear — opal — blue opal.
   Plain or Scalloped edges.)

BEAD & PETAL

BEAD & PETAL

1. *Three pieces.*
   Spooner.
   Covered sugar bowl. Cream pitcher.
2. *Hand lamps.*
3. *Table Lamp.*

BEADED ARCH

BEADED ARCH

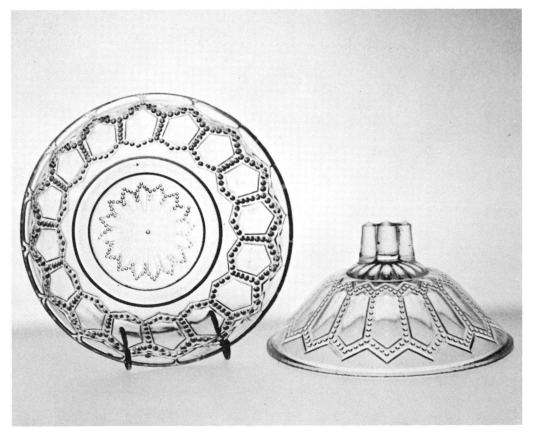

1. *Three pieces*
   Spooner
   Sugar (cover missing)
   Cream Pitcher.

2. *Butter dish - showing base*
   design.

3. *Child's Mug.*

61

DIAMOND MEDALLION COMPORT

LATE JEFFERSON - (Sometimes Mistaken For Rayed Heart)

BLOCK VARIANT COOKIE JAR
(Rare)

SATIN GLASS IN CANADIAN
SILVER PLATE (Burlington)

BEADED BAND

BEADED BAND

1. *Cake Stand dia. 9". Pickle Dish Narrow width 3", length 8", middle width 5". Shallow Footed Bowl dia. 7½"*

2. *Covered Comport ht. dia. 8"*
   Sugar
   Water Pitcher half gallon.

3. *Nappy 2", dia. 4"*

4. *Butter Dish*

   Note. A wide variety of forms — including several sizes bowls and comports, in clear & light amber.

BEADED GRAPE

BEADED GRAPE

1. *4 piece set. Spoon, Butter, Cover-ed Sugar, Cream Pitcher.*

2. *Olive dish sq. 4¼"*
   Celery ht. 5½", Sq. 3¼"
   Toothpick — ht. 2½", Sq. 1¾"
   Nappy Sq. 3¼"

3. *Water Pitcher ½ gallon Round —*
   ht. 10¼"
   Milk Pitcher ½ gallon Sq. Ht. 6½"
   (Note: - Water Pitcher, this is one
   of the few pieces we have seen in
   the round.)

4. *Shallow dish. 10¼" x 7"*
   Shallow dish 7" x 4½"
   Shallow dish. 8¼" x 6"

5. *Salt & Pepper Shakers.*
   Cruet — (Stopper not correct)

6. *Footed Dish, ht. 5½" sq. 6½"*
   Sauce with Flange Sq. 4½"
   Footed Dish Ht. 6", Sq. 7½"
   (Flat dishes not shown).
   6¼"Sq., 7½" Sq., 8¼" Sq.

7. *Goblet.*

BEADED OVAL WINDOW

BEADED OVAL WINDOW

1. *Bread platter ht. 1½", length 12¼", width 8¼".*
2. *Sugar Bowl (lid missing).*
   · *Cream pitcher.*
3. *Open Comport ht. 6½", length 7", width 6".*
   Open Comport ht. 7½", length 8", width 7".

The bread platter shown was first used by members of the old Charlotte Street Methodist Church in Peterborough. Sent by the congregation to the St. James' Church members when that church held services in a tent prior to the building of the church at the corner of Romaine and Aylmer Streets. The plate was used by members of the church from 1908 until 1966 (August 27th) when it was replaced. The plate then became part of a private collection.

BEADED OVAL & FAN NO. 1

BEADED OVAL & FAN NO. 1

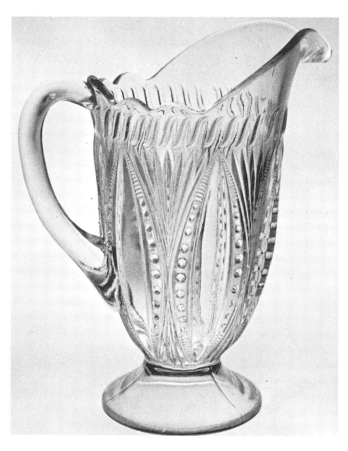

1. Four Piece Set.
   Covered Sugar
   Spoon
   Butter dish ·
   Cream Pitcher

2. Cakestand.
   ht. - dia. 9".

3. Nappies.
   dia. 4¼".
   Fruit Bowl.
   dia. 8¼".

4. Water Pitcher.
   Half gallon.

BEADED OVAL & FAN No. 2

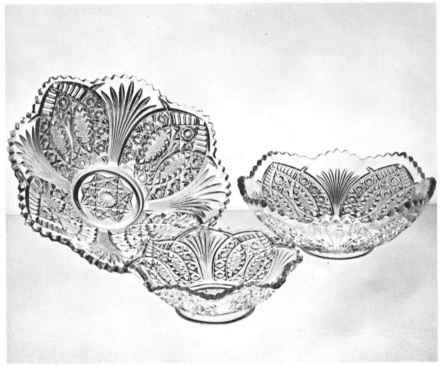

BEADED OVAL & FAN NO. 2

1. *Banana dish footed. ht. 7½". Length 9¼".*
   Bowl or nut dish. ht. 4¼", dia. 5¼"
   Basket. ht. to top of handle. 6", length 7½".

2. *Covered Sugar and Spoon.*

3. *Footed Jelly. ht. 5", dia. 5¾".*
   Shallow bowl 2¾", dia. 8½".
   Footed Bowl. ht. 6¾", dia. 8¼".

4. *Wine variants. dia. 2¼", 2⅛" dia. 2½",*
   all ht. 3¼".

5. *Squared Bowl. Ht. 3½", diam. 11¼".*

6. *Tumbler Ht. 4½" & half gallon Water Pit-*
   cher Ht. 7½".

7. *Celery - ht. 6", dia. 4½", Toothpick - ht. 2¼",*
   Cruet - 7½".

8. *Bowl. ht. 3¼", dia. 10¼".*
   Bowl. ht. 2½", dia. 7½".
   Bowl. ht. 3¼", dia. 9".

9. *Miniature 4 piece set. Sugar 2¼" Ht.*

10. *Base Design.*

BLOCK

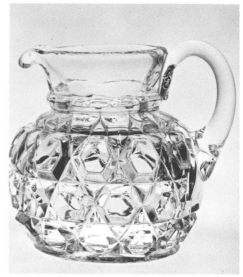

BLOCK

1. Nappy. dia. 4¼".
   Bowl. ht. 2¾", dia. 4½".
   Syrup Jug. ht. 4¾".
2. Cream Pitcher (Burlington Mark.) ht. 4½".
3. Sugar Shaker.
4. Tumbler.
   Water Pitcher. Half gallon ht. 9".

5. Bowl. ht. 2½", dia. 2½".
6. Cream Pitcher. ht. 4", dia. 2½".
   Syrup Jug. ht. 6¾".
   Cream Pitcher. ht. 3¼", dia. 3".
7. Water Pitcher. Half gallon ht. 8".
8. Decanter with wine glasses and matching tray.

BURLINGTON PITCHER (*Etched*)

CANADIAN

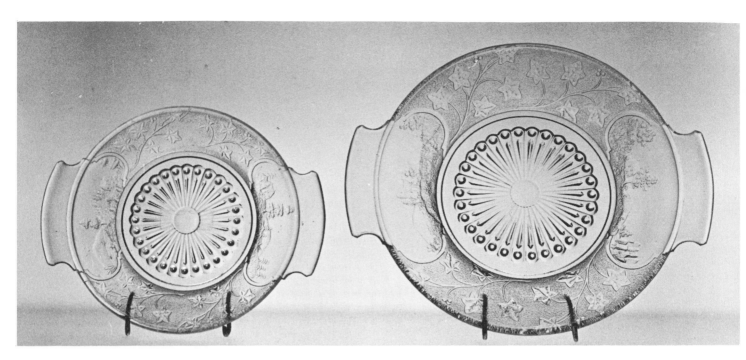

CANADIAN

1. *Covered comport.*

2. *Plate dia. 8" with handles 10" across. Plate dia. 6".*

3. *Water pitcher. Half gallon.*
   Cream pitcher.

4. *Celery.*

5. *Covered bowl — flange handles. ht. 7¼", dia. 8".*
   (note, scene with sailing ship. Identical to that depicted on the CAPE COD goblet.)

6. *Nappy ht. 2½". dia. 3½".*
   Nappy ht. 1¼". dia 3½".

7. *Covered Sugar.*

8. *Covered pickle jar. ht. 6½".*

CANADIAN DRAPE

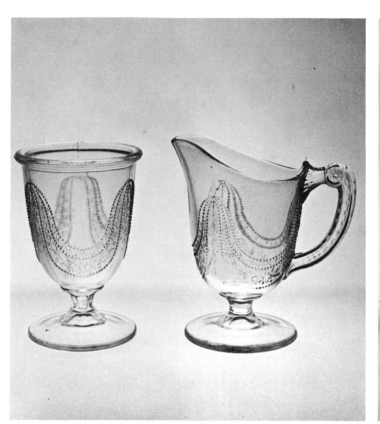

**CANADIAN
DRAPE**

1. *Sugar bowl.*

   Cream pitcher

2. *Nappy dia. 3½".*

   Celery ht. 8½".

3. *Open comport ht. 8", dia. 8".*

4. *Cake Stand. ht. 7", dia. 9¼".*

5. *Water pitcher. ht. 8½".*

*Note — this pattern is most attractive. Made in full
range of tablewares and lamps.*

77

CANADIAN FLANGE

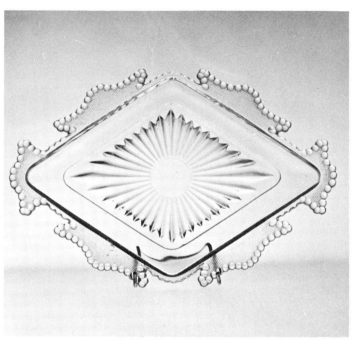

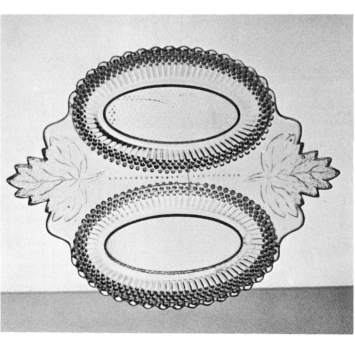

CANADIAN FLANGE

1. *Cream Pitcher.*

2. *Relish dish.*

3. *Butter dish - Maple Leaf flanges.*

4. *Relish dish - double ovals - Concordia flange.*

    Note - Flange pattern is hard to find in perfect condition.

CANADIAN HORSESHOE

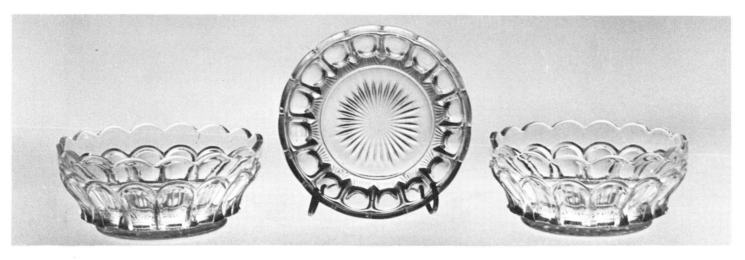

CANADIAN HORSESHOE

1. *Three Nappies. ht. 2", dia. 4".*

2. *Spooner.*
   Cream Pitcher.

3. *Sugar (lid missing).*

4. *Fruit Bowl, dia. 9".*

CANADIAN THISTLE

CANADIAN THISTLE

1. *Basket. ht. 4½", length 6", width 4½".*
2. *Swung Vase. ht. 10". Swung Vase. ht. 12".*
3. *Square Honey dish 5" x 5".*
4. *Cream Pitcher. Butter dish. Spoon. (Sugar not shown)*
5. *Nappy. ht. 2½", dia. 6". Nappy. ht. 2", dia. 7". Bowl. ht. 4", dia. 4½".*
6. *Plate. dia. 8". Plate. dia. 10¾".*
7. *Nappy. ht. 1½", dia. 4¼". Wine. ht. 4", dia. 2¼". Sundae. ht. 4¼", dia. 3¾". Footed Nappy. ht. 2", dia. 3¼".*
8. *Footed dish. ht. 4¾", dia. 4¾". Footed Sweetmeat. ht. 3¼", dia. 3¼". Footed Bowl. ht. 5", dia. 5", depth 2¼".*
9. *Vase. ht. 6". Large Vase. ht. 9". Vase. ht. 6½".*
10. *Tall Celery. ht. 4½". Footed salts. ht. 1½". Vinegar or oil. ht. 3½" (stopper incorrect).*
11. *Water Pitcher half gallon. ht. 7¾".*
   American pieces have Higbee trademark impressed on them.

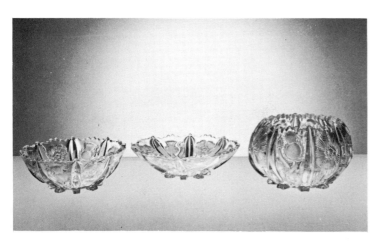

CHAIN WITH STAR

CHAIN WITH STAR

1. *Spoon, Sugar (lid missing), Butter, Cream.*

2. *Plate, 11¼" including handles, Nappies, ht. 1½", dia 4", Bowl footed, ht. 4", dia. 9½".*

3. *Low covered comport. ht. 8", dia. 7". High covered comport ht. 12", dia. 9".*

4. *High covered comport. ht. 10½", dia. 7". Low covered comport. ht. 9", dia. 9".*

5. *Shallow bowl. dia. 7½". Cake Stand. ht. 5", dia. 9½". Oval dish wd. 5¾", lg. 7½".*

6. *Goblet, Pitcher, ht. 9¼". All forms of tableware made.*

CHANDELIER

CHANDELIER

1. *Footed Bowl.* $7\frac{1}{2}$" *ht.,* 9" *dia.*

2. *Four Piece Set. Butter, Sugar, Cream, Spoon.*

3. *Goblet, Tumbler, Water Pitcher, ht.* $9\frac{1}{2}$".

4. *Master Salt. ht.* 2", *dia.* $2\frac{3}{4}$".
   Celery. ht. $6\frac{1}{4}$", *dia.* 4".

5. *Bowl. ht.* $3\frac{1}{4}$", *dia.* 8".
   Nappy. ht. 2", *dia.* 4".
   Nappy. ht. $2\frac{1}{4}$", *dia.* $3\frac{1}{4}$".

*Note. A great variety of forms were made in this pattern -
several sizes of pitchers, comports, fancy bowls and
salvers - also master salts and shakers.*

85

COLONIAL

COLONIAL

1. 2 Cream Pitchers.
   Sugar bowl.
2. Bowl. ht. 3½". dia. 7½".
   Footed salver. ht. 6", dia. 8".
3. Ice cream dish.
   Footed Sundae.
   Banana Split.
4. Covered butter tub. ht. 8", dia. 4½".
   Covered butter tub. ht. 5¼", dia. 4½".
   (note size of covers and difference in size of finials)
5. Covered Comport. ht. 10". dia. 7".
   Oval dish. ht. 2". Length 10".
   Oval dish. ht. 2", Length 8¼".
6. Covered Cream Pitcher
   Covered Sugar Bowl.
   (Note Chippendale handle on creamer also difference in size of finials)
7. Water Pitcher. ht. 8½".
   (popular restaurant and hotel ware.)

COLOSSUS

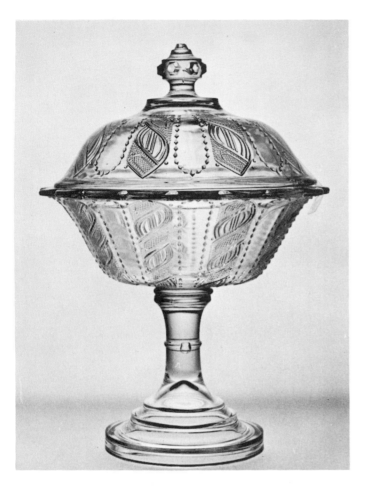

COLOSSUS

1. *Covered Comport.*
   ht. 10½", *dia.* 6½".

2. *Cream Pitcher.*

3. *Fruit bowl (shallow)*
   dia. 8".

Note - full range of table wares made, foot and finial similar to Beaded Oval and Scroll and Buckle with Diamond Band.

CONCORDIA MAPLE LEAF

CONCORDIA MAPLE LEAF

1. *Concordia Plate dia.* 10¼".

2. *Flanged Maple Leaf Plate dia.* 10¼".

3. *Maple Leaf - single leaf centre dia.* 10¼".

4. *Flanged Butter dish.*

Note - other forms of this pattern known. Four piece setting. Pickle dishes - Cheese bell - Nappies.

CORINTHIAN

CORINTHIAN

1. *Covered Comport. ht. 10½",*
   Dia. 7½".
   Covered Comport. ht. 11½",
   Dia. 8½".
   (note foot. This is identical to
   that of RIBBED BAND.)

2. *Open Sugar.*
   Footed Celery. ht. 10".

3. *Covered Comport. ht. 11½",*
   dia. 7½".

   (Note—forms indicate a full
   range of table ware was made.)

CROSS

CROSS

1. *Covered Sugar.*
   ht. 6", dia. 4".

2. *Open Comport.*
   ht. 8", dia. 10½".

3. *Vinegar Cruet.*
   ht. 6".
   Nappy or Pickle
   dish. dia. 6".

4. *Fruit Stand.*
   ht. 8½", dia. 9".

5. *Celery tall.*
   ht. 6¾", square 4".
   Note. Complete
   range of table
   wares made in this
   pattern also design
   used on lamps.

DAHLIA

DAHLIA

1. *Three Pieces.*
   Sugar bowl (lid missing).
   Spooner.
   Cream Pitcher.

2. *Plate. dia. 10½".*

3. *Water Pitcher. Half gallon.*

4. *Oval Platter. Length 11".*

DAISY & DEPRESSED BUTTON

DAISY & DEPRESSED BUTTON

1. *Oval Pickle dish ht. 1½", length 7"*
   Cake Stand ht. 6½", dia. 9"
   Oval Pickle dish ht. 6½", length 9"

2. *Milk Pitcher ht. 8½"*
   Water pitcher half gallon ht. 9½"

3. *Butter dish - (blue)*

4. *Fruit bowl ht. 3¼", dia. 8½"*
   Nappy ht. 1¼", dia. 4"
   Nappy footed ht. 2¼", dia. 4"
   Footed bowl ht. 8", dia. 8½"

5. *Covered Sugar Jar*

6. *Breakfast (or individual) Sugar bowl*
   Breakfast (or individual) Cream pitcher (light blue)

Note - Popular pattern, many forms colours - çlear, blue, dark and light, green, yellow, amber.

95

DAISY WITH CROSS BAR

DAISY WITH CROSS BAR

1. *Nappies - ht. 2¾", dia. 4".*
   Vinegar Cruet 9".

2. *Three pieces*
   Spooner
   Covered Sugar
   Cream Pitcher

3. *Goblet*
   Water Pitcher - half gallon ht. 8".

4. *Covered Comport - ht. 8½", dia. 8".*
   Covered Comport - ht. 11½", dia. 7¾".

5. *Fruit bowl - ht. 4", dia. 7¼".*
   Open Comport - ht. 7½", dia. 8¼".
   Note - the forms photographed are
   amber - clear and blue also made.

DAISY AND X BAND

DAISY & X BAND

1. *Open Comport ht. 7", dia. 8¼"; Footed Nappy ht. 2¼", dia 3¾"; Large Nappy ht. 1¾", dia. 5¾"; Nappy ht. 1¼", dia. 4"; Low footed Nappy ht. 1¾", dia. 5".*

2. *Sundae dish footed - Cream Pitcher.*

3. *Basket length 5¾".*

4. *Three pieces - Spooner, Covered Sugar bowl, Cream Pitcher.*

5. *Plate dia. 10¾"; Fruit bowl ht. 3", dia. 4"; Fruit bowl ht. 4", dia. 5". (Note design in centre of Cake Plate)*

6. *Celery ht. 5½", dia. 4"; Toothpick holder ht. 2", dia. 2"; Nappy ht. 2½", dia. 5".*

7. *Fruit Salver. (rayed centre) ht. 6¾", dia. 8½".*

8. *Fruit bowl dia. 8"; Pair footed Nappies ht. 2", dia. 5". Note - wide choice of forms - colour - clear- blue - amber.*

DAISY VARIANTS

1. *Belmont Daisy Water Pitcher (clear).*

2. *Daisy Pitcher - (Amber).*

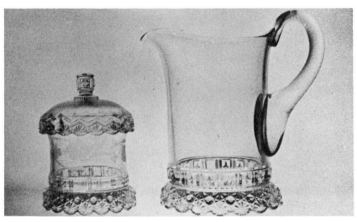

3. *Daisy with Petticoat Band. Covered Sugar & Water Pitcher.*

4. *Daisy Hat - Amber - ht. 3½".*

5. *Daisy with Petticoat Band, Fruit Bowl, ht. 3½", dia. 7".*

6. *Daisy Sugar & Creamer (amber), from Breakfast set.*

DAISY WITH THUMBPRINT

Comport (amber), ht. 10½", dia. 6½".

Finger Bowl, ht. 3½", dia. 4½". Celery (amber).

GRAPE & FESTOON WITH SHIELD

Nappy dia. 4".

NOTE - owing to many patterns being little known to collectors, only a few examples were available to photograph. We regret that we are unable to arrange patterns in strict Alphabetical order.

Sugar - Cover missing.
Cream Pitcher.

DEER & DOG

DEER & DOG

1. *Low covered Comport.*

2. *High Covered Comport - ht. 13", dia. 8¼".*

3. *Spooner.*

4. *Low Covered Comport - ht. 7½", long 6".*

5. *Cream Pitcher - ht. 7".*

   Sugar bowl - ht. 9", dia. 4½".

6. *High Covered Comport - ht. 12", long 9", wide 7".*

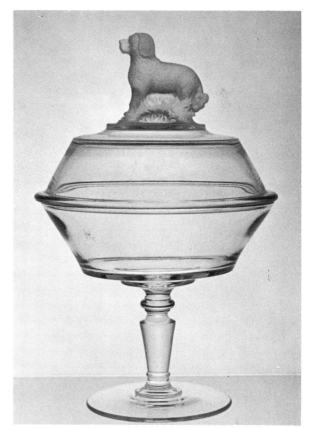

DOMINION

DOMINION

1. *Honey dish, dia. 2½" approx.*
   Plate, dia. 10". ·
   Footed nappy, ht. 2½", dia. 3½".

2. *Footed bowl, ht. 7", dia. 7".*

3. *Butter dish, etched.*

4. *Four of five sizes in candy jars.*
   15", 13½", 11¾" - 8".
   made for R. T. Watson, Confectioner,
   Toronto.

5. *Candy jar, pear shaped, 4 lb. size.*

6. *Candy jar, square shaped.*

7. *Footed nappy, dia. 4".*

DIAMOND MEDALLION

DIAMOND MEDALLION

1. *Water Pitcher. half gallon ht. 9"; Cream Pitcher. ht. 6¼"*
2. *Footed Nappy. ht. 2¾", dia. 6½".*
   Cake Plate dia. 10"; Spooner ht. 4½", dia. 3¼".
3. *Cake Stand ht. 4", dia. 8½".*
   Comport (open) ht. 7½", dia. 7".
4. *Covered Comport ht. 8", dia 5½". ..Goblet.*

ESTHER

1. *Water Pitcher, half gallon.* (*Burlington Mark*)
2. *Covered Comport.*

COMMENT

During the past year many patterns not previously listed as Canadian made have been identified by the BURLINGTON MARK. This mark was brought to the attention of the collector and specifically described by John R. Sheeler in article six of the Burlington Glass Site series, Canadian (antiques) Collector, November, 1968.

Mr. Sheeler and his colleague Mr. Peter Behn are foremost in the field of research on the history of Canadian Glass. As a result of their efforts many new facts have been brought to light and some misconceptions corrected. Messrs. Sheeler and Behn have a broad scope of endeavour, having worked for a long period to uncover pertinent facts. Research has led them to various archives, collectors home, and dealers stores. They have been active participants in several 'digs'. It is hoped that in the not too far future the results of this combined effort will be published and available to all.

FEATHER BAND

FEATHER BAND

1. *Four Piece Set.*
   Sugar (lid missing)
   Butter dish.
   Cream pitcher. footed.
   Spoon.

2. *Water pitcher, half gallon ht. 8½".*
   Water pitcher, half gallon ht. 8½".
   Note differences in water pitchers. Panels on second

pitcher match four piece set and cake stand. First pitcher has more relationship to the plate and nappy shown in picture No. 4 — possibly two separate sets.

3. *Cake Stand. ht. 4½", Dia. 8½".*
   Cake stand (lying on side) ht. 4½", dia. 10".

4. *Shallow footed salver, ht. 5", dia. 10".*
   Nappy, dia. 4¼".
   Plate. dia. 5½".

FILLY OR NOTCHED
BULL'S EYE

Fruit Bowl dia. 8".
Cream pitcher.

Celery vase.

FISHSCALE AMERICAN

Plate dia. 9".

Comport Ht. 8¼", dia. 8¼".

FLOWER & QUILL

1. Covered butter dish.

2. Celery Vase.
   colours, pale green, pale yellow,
   pale blue.

FROSTED FLOWER BAND

1. Covered Butter dish.

2. Water pitcher, half gallon.

   Note - this pattern like many other flower patterns has been re-produced.

GOOD LUCK

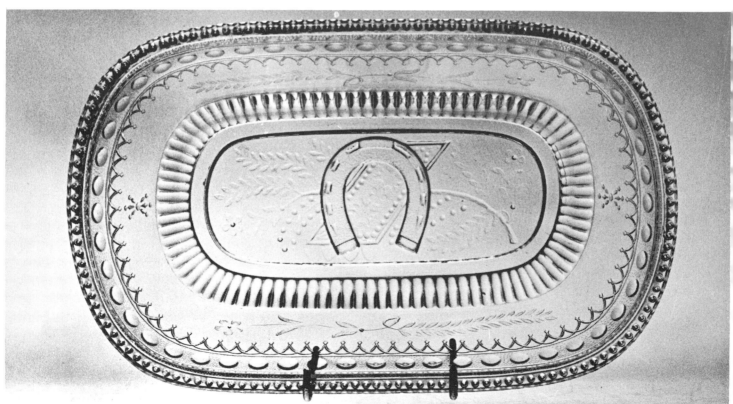

GOOD LUCK

1. *Bread Platter.*

2. *Oval dish - ht. 2¼", width 5¾", length 9¼"*

3. *Butter dish - cover missing.*

4. *Cake Stand. ht. 6½", dia. 9".*

5. *Cover Comport. ht. 12", dia. 8".*

6. *Water Pitcher half gallon - ht. 9".*

NOTE

We regret we are unable to adhere to strict alphabetical order in any section of "Pattern and Form".

GREEK KEY & WEDDING RING

GREEK KEY & WEDDING RING

1. *Spooner*
   Sugar - cover missing
   Cream Pitcher

2. *Butter dish showing base design.*

3. *Fruit bowl ht. 3", dia. 8".*
   Nappy ht. 1½", dia. 4".

   Note - Colours clear, blue opalescent, Green opalescent.

   We have not seen Water Pitcher - Tumbler or Goblet yet.

HONEYCOMB

HONEYCOMB

1. *Water pitcher half gallon ht. 9"*
   Note - unusual form and beautiful handle.

2. *Fruit bowl footed ht. 7", dia. 8½"*

3. *Open Comport - ht. 10", dia. 7"*

Note colours seen - clear - pale green - amber.

These forms indicate other tablewares made.

JACOB'S LADDER

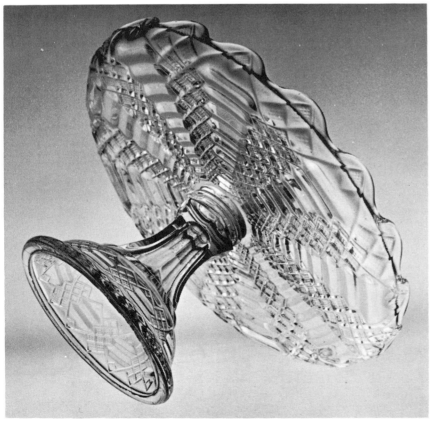

JACOB'S LADDER

1. *Bread Platter.*
2. *Cake Stand. ht. 5", dia. 9¼".*
3. *Covered Comport. ht. 10", dia. 6" (note finial different to one on sugar.)*
4. *Celery. ht. 9". Nappy. dia. 3½". Nappy. dia. 4½".*
5. *Cream pitcher. ht. 6¼" footed.*
   Water Pitcher. ht. 10" applied handle.
   (Note difference in handles.)
6. *Covered Sugar — (note finial — Maltese Cross impressed on finial not free standing as on comport.)*

LATTICE

LATTICE

1. *Plate dia. 10".*
   Footed bowl ht. 7¼", dia. 8¾".
2. *Spooner.*
   Cream pitcher.
3. *Bread platter.*
4. *Footed bowl deep, dia. 7½".*
   Footed bowl shallow, dia. 8½".
   Note - base patterns vary greatly but four petals in square
   seems part of every piece seen.

LEAF AND DART

LEAF AND DART

1. *Four Piece Set Spooner. Covered Sugar. Butter Dish. Cream Pitcher.*

2. *Milk Pitcher (one quart).*
3. *Celery Vase.*

LILY - OF - THE - VALLEY

LILY - OF - THE - VALLEY

1. *Three Pieces - Spooner. Sugar Bowl (lid missing). Cream Pitcher.*
   Note. This is the three legged version. The acorn pendant at base looks odd — the pattern seems to belong with the Nova Scotia designs.

2. *Pickle dish - Scoop Shape. ht. 1¼", long 8", wide 4".*

3. *Water Pitcher. Half gallon - ht. 8½".*

4. *Celery - ht. 8".*

5. *Spooner - from the other variation of the pattern.*

6. *Butter dish covered - belongs with Spooner.*

LION

LION PLATTER

LOOP & STAR

LOOP and STAR PLATE Dia. 7"

LOOP and STAR BUTTER DISH

LOOP & PILLAR

LOOP & PILLAR

1. *Four Piece Set*
   Cream pitcher; Covered butter; Covered Sugar; Spooner.

2. *Bride's Basket - Canadian Silver Plate.*

3. *Fruit bowl from silver plated stand ht. 5", dia. 8½".*
   Note - this pattern similar to BEAD & PETAL in design but more elaborate in form.

MAPLE LEAF

MAPLE LEAF

1. *Four piece set. Spooner. Covered Sugar. Butter dish.*
   Cream pitcher.
2. *Open Comport. ht. 7¼", dia. 7½".*
   Cake stand. ht. 5", dia. 9½".
3. *Footed bowl. ht. 8", dia. 10½".*
4. *Fruit bowl. ht. 3½", dia. 8½".*
5. *Footed bowl, fluted. ht. 7½", dia. 10".*

6. *Water pitcher, half gallon.*

Note. Maple leaf seen in green, opal white and blue.
Made in many forms but have not found jam or pickle
jars, any type of cruet in it. Matching tumbler and goblet
may have been made but those seen bearing maple leaves
do not relate to the table wares.

MINERVA

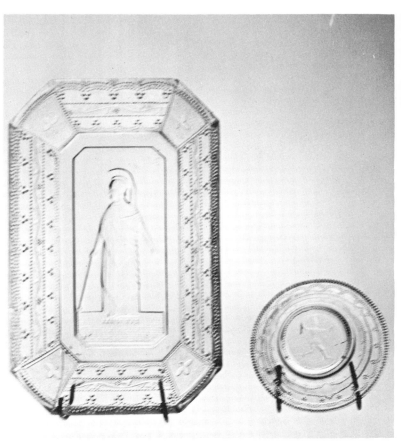

MINERVA

1. *Water pitcher. ht. 9½".*

2. *Shallow dish. ht. 2", width 6", length 9".*
   Honey dish. dia. 3¾".

3. *Cake stand. ht. 7", dia. 11".*

4. *Milk Pitcher (note difference in shape and ornamentation on handle also shape of spout and rim)*

5. *Covered Comport. ht. 9½". dia. 8".*

6. *Footed Bowl. ht. 5", dia. 8".*

7. *Pickle insert (cover missing)*

127

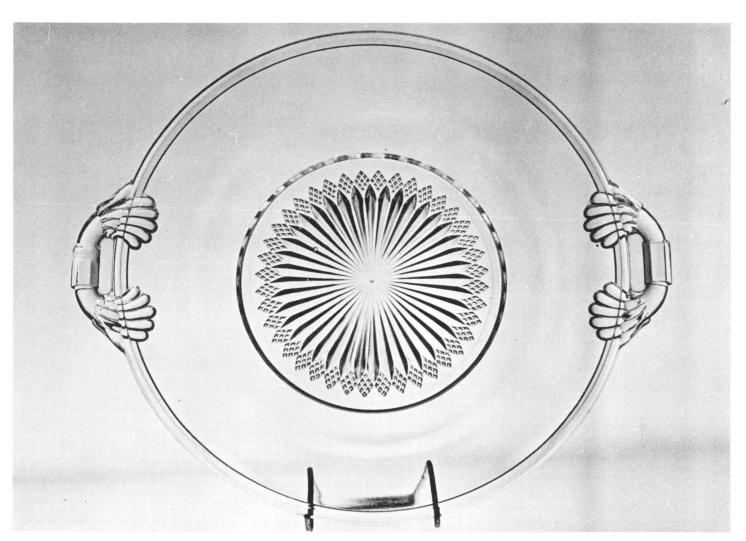

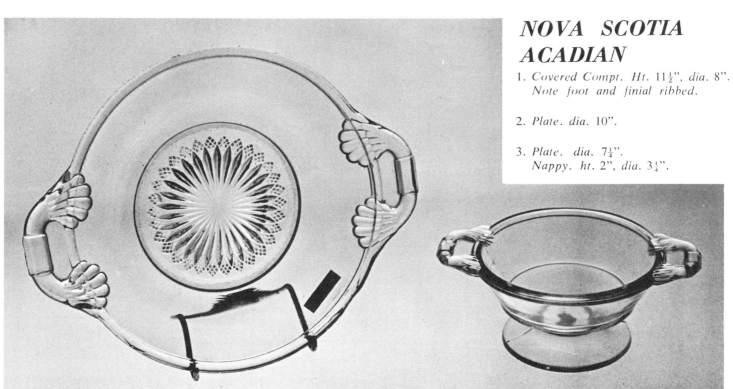

NOVA SCOTIA
ACADIAN

1. *Covered Compt. Ht. 11½", dia. 8".
Note foot and finial ribbed.*

2. *Plate. dia. 10".*

3. *Plate. dia. 7¼".
Nappy. ht. 2", dia. 3¼".*

GOBLETS

NS BUTTONS & BOWS

*NS BUTTONS & BOWS
CORDIAL*

NS DIAMOND RAY

NS RIBBED BAND

NS GRAPE & VINE

NS STAR FLOWER

130

NOVA SCOTIA BUTTONS & BOWS

1. *Sugar Jar Covered.*

2. *Water Pitcher. Half gallon.*

Note. Nappy not shown. ht. 1½″, dia. 3¼″. Full range of tablewares made.

NOVA SCOTIA CENTENNIAL

1. *Covered Comport - ht. 11¾", dia. 8".*

2. *Cream Pitcher ht. 6".*
   Water Pitcher half gallon ht. 9".

3. *Butter dish (cover missing).*

4. *Cake stand ht. 5¼", dia. 9¾".*
   Open Comport ht. 7", dia. 7¾".

5. *Open Comport ht. 6½", dia. 10" depth of bowl 3".*

6. *Spooner.*

   Open Comport ht. 8", dia. 8½". Comports vary considerably.

   Sugar jar (lid missing).

133

NOVA SCOTIA CROWN

NOVA SCOTIA CROWN

1. Cheese bell.

2. Tumbler with carafe.

3. Oil and vinegar on tray with mustard pot (stoppers and lid missing)

4. Footed bowl. ht. 7½", dia 8".
   Footed bowl. ht. 6½", dia. 7½".

5. Covered comport. ht. 10", dia. 5½" note made in several sizes.

6. Three pieces. Covered sugar, etched. Spooner etched. Cream pitcher, etched.
   note butter dish not shown looks like small crown on plate.

7. Nappy, dia. 4" note made in several sizes.
   This pattern similar to BALL, McKee Glass Company advertised Vinegar cruet 1894 catalogue, stopper Maltese Cross. See Kamm-Wood, BOOK ONE, page 28. CROWN also made at Burlington Glass Factory.

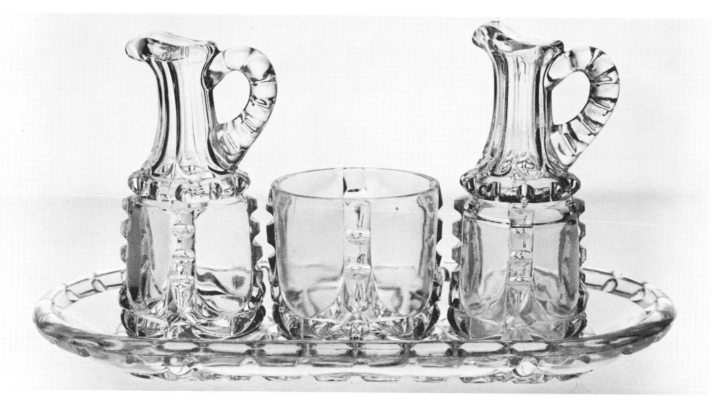

NOVA SCOTIA HOBNAIL

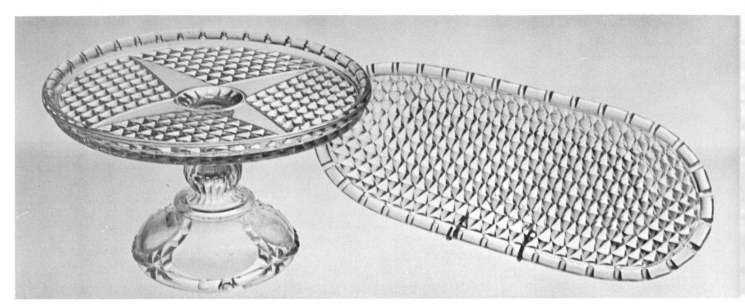

NOVA SCOTIA HOBNAIL WITH NOVA SCOTIA CROWN

1. *Cake stand, ht. 6¾", dia. 10½".*
   Oval bread tray. length 15½", width 6".
Note - these forms listed as Hobnail by the Nova Scotia
   Museum but would seem to belong to the N.S. Crown
   pattern. Foot of cake stand the same as N.S. Crown

comporis, the plate of cake stand same as base of N.S.
Crown butter dish. Rim of bread tray same as edges of
N.S. Crown pieces.

2. *Nova Scotia Crown covered comport.*
3. *Nova Scotia Crown Cookie jar. (rare).*

NOVA SCOTIA DIAMOND

NOVA SCOTIA DIAMOND

1. *Nappy. ht. 2", dia. 4". Footed bowl ht. 5¾", dia. 7¼". Honey or butter pat dia. 4¼".*

2. *Sugar Jar (covered).*

3. *Butter dish.*
   Note. This pattern was used on many forms including articles for the dressing table.

NOVA SCOTIA DIAMOND RAY

NOVA SCOTIA
DIAMOND RAY

1. *Footed dish. ht. 5½", dia. 9".*
   Footed bowl. ht. 6½", dia. 7½".
   Covered comport. ht. 9¾", dia. 6½".

2. *Water pitcher half gallon.*
   Goblet.

3. *Four piece set.*
   Spooner.
   Covered sugar.
   Butter dish. Note all butter dishes seen have CEN-TENNIAL base.
   Cream pitcher.

4. *Cake stand. ht. 4½", dia. 9¼".*
   Fruit bowl. ht. 2½", dia. 9½".
   Plate. dia. 8½".
   Footed comport. ht. 7", dia. 7¼".
   wide variety of forms, several sizes in plates, bowls, comports and cakestands. Footed pieces seen are the same as on NOVA SCOTIA CROWN.

138

NOVA SCOTIA GRAPE & VINE

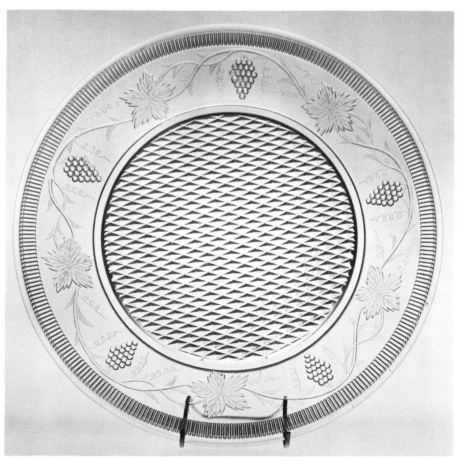

NOVA SCOTIA
GRAPE & VINE

1. *Four piece set*
   Covered Sugar bowl
   Butter dish
   Spooner
   Cream pitcher

2. *Fruit bowl ht. 3", dia. 7"*
   Covered Comport ht. 10½", dia. 6½"
   Open Comport ht. 6", dia. 6"

3. *Water Pitcher - half gallon ht. 9"*

4. *Cheese Bell ht. 8", dia. 6½"*

5. *Bread Plate - dia. 10¾"*

NOVA SCOTIA RASPBERRY

NOVA SCOTIA RASPBERRY

1. *Two Nappies with flange dia. 4¾".*
   Plate. . dia. 6".

2. *Plate. dia. 10", has flange both sides.*
   Note. Plates also in 9" and some
   have small thumb hold curved on one
   flange believed to be on the Ontario
   made pieces only.

NOVA SCOTIA RASPBERRY & SHIELD

NOVA SCOTIA
RASPBERRY & SHIELD

1. *Three pieces. Spooner. Sugar bowl - lid missing. Cream pitcher.*

2. *Covered pickle or jam (note markings on sides of jar - not leaves and berry as on cream pitcher - Ht. 5¾", dia. 3¼".*

3. *Butter dish. Note could also be used with N.S. Raspberry.*

NOVA SCOTIA RIBBED BAND

NOVA SCOTIA RIBBED BAND

1. *Four piece set. Spooner, Covered Sugar, Butter dish, Cream pitcher.*

2. *Covered Comport. Ht. 10½", dia. 6½".*
   Not shown covered comports — dia. 6" - 7" and 8".

3. *Cheese bell. Plain - some are etched.*

   Not shown - Water pitcher half gallon - bread platter large 11".

CANADIAN GLASS
IN COLOUR

1. *Selection of forms in Coin Dot, Lattice and Swirl - Burlington Glass Works.*

2. *Pitchers illustrating some of the colours used for pattern glass.*
   Opal glass was also used for special orders.
   — Ontario Factories.

3. *Maple Leaf Tablewares. (green) also made in opal white and blue.*

4. *Iris with Meander - colour Vaseline to opal cream - Jefferson-Dominion, Toronto.*
   Some Jefferson patterns are now being manufactured by Davidson Glass Co., Newcastle-on-Tyne, England.

1.	2.
3.	4.

Key to Coloured Glass.
Plate No. 2.

NOVA SCOTIA RIBBON AND STAR

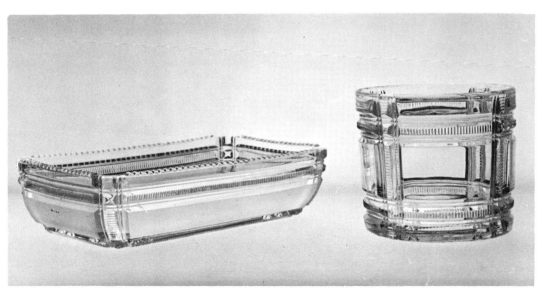

NOVA SCOTIA RIBBON AND STAR

1. *Water Pitcher half gallon.*

2. *Nappy. dia. 4".*
   Pickle or Jam Jar. Ht. 6",
   dia. 3".

3. *Pickle dish frosted sides.*
   Ht. 2¼", long 8¼", wide 5¼".
   Master Salt.

NOVA SCOTIA STARFLOWER

NOVA SCOTIA STARFLOWER

1. *Three pieces. Sugar bowl (cover missing), Butter dish, dewdrop base. Cream pitcher.*
   Note. The difference between this and the next set. Many variations are found in the Starflower design.

2. *Four piece set. Covered sugar, finial variation. Butter dish, waffle base. Spooner. Cream pitcher.*

3. *Water pitcher. Half gallon.*

4. *Covered Comport. Plain foot. ht. 10½", dia. 9".*

5. *Butter dish, showing waffle base.*

6. *Footed bowl, note the ornate foot. ht. 8", dia. 9".*

7. *Cake stand. ht. 7", dia. 8¼".*

NOVA SCOTIA TANDEM

1. *Plate dia. 10".*
   Plate dia. 6".
2. *Celery Vase.*

NOVA SCOTIA FLORAL

1. *Photograph includes Square Marsh Pink Relish tray collected as Floral.*
   Covered Floral Butter dish. Floral Cream Pitcher.

NOVA SCOTIA TASSEL & CREST

NOVA SCOTIA TASSEL & CREST

1. *Covered Sugar. Covered Comport Ht. 11", dia. 8". Cream pitcher.*

2. *Water pitcher. Half gallon.*

3. *Butter dish.*

   Not shown. Nappy. dia. 3¾".

NOVA SCOTIA VICTORIA
COMMEMORATIVE 1837-1887

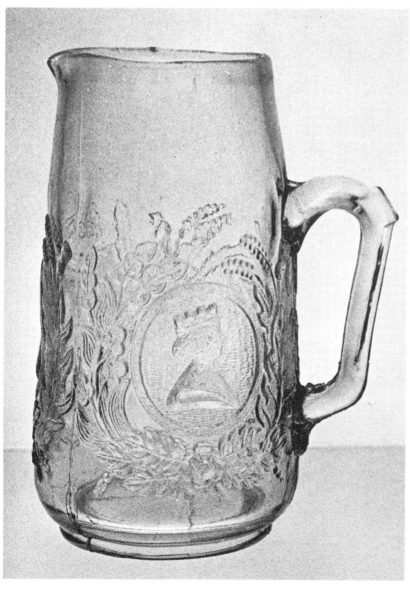

N. S. Victoria Commemorative
1837 - 1867

1. *Plate with single head - wreath dia. 10"*
   Plate with single head - rayed dia. 10"

2. *Plate with two heads - rayed dia. 10"*

3. *Plate with two heads - wreath dia. 10"*

4. *Four piece set single head - shield*
   Cream Pitcher
   Sugar Jar
   Sugar Jar (cover missing)
   Spooner

5. *Water Pitcher - half gallon single head -*
   Medallion (not the same series)

6. *Covered bowl*

NUGGET, EARLY & LATE

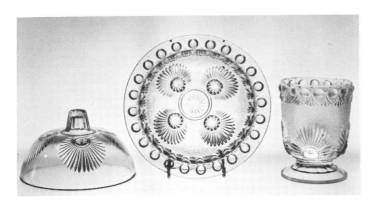

NUGGET EARLY & LATE

1. *Butter dish*
   Sugar - (cover missing) (Late)

2. *Plate dia. 10" (early)*

3. *Tumbler amber (early)*
   Tumbler clear (late)

4. *Water Pitcher half gallon ht. $7\frac{3}{4}$" (early)*

5. *Four piece set*
   Sugar bowl; Spooner ; Butter dish; Cream Pitcher - (late)

6. *Water Pitcher - half gallon ht.   (late)*

7. *Cake stand dia. $9\frac{1}{4}$" - (comes in several sizes)*

8. *Covered Comport ht. $10\frac{1}{2}$", dia $8\frac{1}{4}$"*

9. *Fruit Bowl - dia. $7\frac{3}{4}$"*

Note - comports, fruit bowls, nappies, cakestands in several
   sizes - scalloped or plain edges - colours - clear - amber
   - green and blue.

101

1. *Plate for bread. Dia. 11¼".*

2. *Celery Vase*

3. *Three pieces - Spooner; Sugar (cover missing); Cream pitcher.*

4. *Covered Comport. Ht. 10½", dia. 7¼"*

5. *Water pitcher. half gallon ht. 9½".*

6. *Plate dia. 8"; Plate dia. 7".*

7. *Nappy ht. 1¼", dia. 4".*

Note - this is one of the patterns where the water pitcher has been found with the Burlington Mark on the tab of the handle. All of these Burlington made patterns are of high quality glass - clear - bright - and graceful in line.

101 - One-o-one. So called because of the pattern - original name not known.

NO. 204 WARE

NO. 204 WARE

1. *Four piece set: Covered Sugar, Spoon, Butter dish, Cream pitcher - Note: this set is a dark green.*

2. *Water pitcher half gallon. ht. 9".*
   Fruit bowl. ht. 3¼", Dia. 8¼".
   Open Comport. ht. 7½", Dia. 4¾".

3. *Open Comport Squared top. ht. 8", dia. 9".*

   Nappy matching. ht. 1¾", Dia. 4¾".

   Note: Comes in a wide variety of bowls, comports and Nappies - have not seen a covered comport. Green, Amber - Opal (rare).

1883 PATTERN

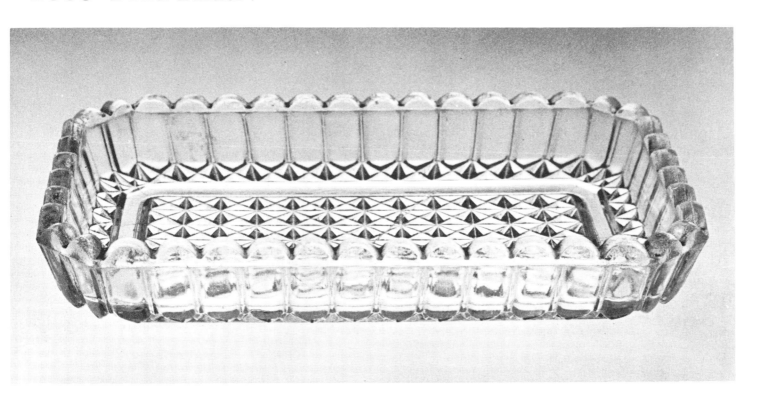

1883 PATTERN

1. *Candy dish 10" length, range in sizes 7", 8", 9", 10", 11", both clear and coloured glass - made with and without handles - sometimes bearing the name of the customer.*

2. *Cake Stand.*
   See Stevens Canadian Glass 1825 - 1925 page 180.

PALMETTE

PALMETTE

1. Goblet. ht. 6½".
   Water Pitcher half gallon. ht. 9".

2. Covered Sugar. ht. 7½", dia. 4¼".
   Cream Pitcher. ht. 6".

3. Honey dish. dia. 3¼".
   Nappy. dia. 4½".

4. Spooner
   Covered Comport. ht. 10", dia. 7¼".
       Sugar (cover missing)

5. Open Comport. ht. 8".

6. Footed bowl - ht. 5½", dia. 8".

PANELLED FORGET-ME-NOT

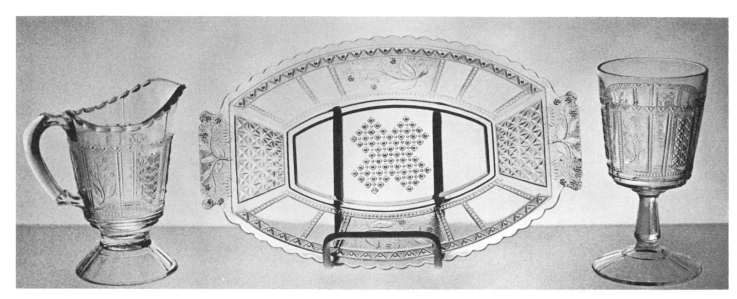

PANELLED FORGET-ME-NOT

1. *Cream Pitcher.*
   Bread Platter - ht. 2", long 9¾", wide 5½".
   Goblet.

2. *Covered Comport ht. 10", dia 8½".*

3. *Footed Bowl - ht. 6½", dia 9½".*

PICKET

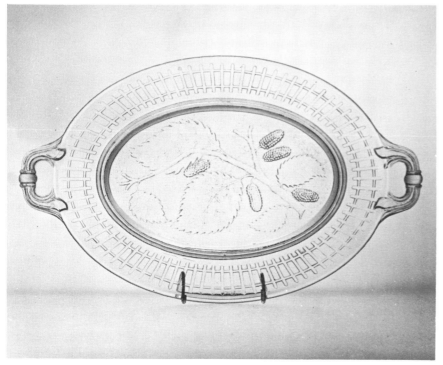

PICKET

1. *Bread Platter - Pussy Willow design on base. length 13",*
   width 8".

2. *Water Pitcher. half gallon.*

3. *Open Comport. ht. 7", dia. 7".*

4. *Open Comport. ht. 5¾", dia. 6".*

   Covered dish. ht. 6", dia. 6½".

   Note - comes in variety of forms including open salt

   1¼" x 2" individual salts and goblets.

PILLOW ENCIRCLED · BURLINGTON (*Etched*)

PLEAT & PANEL

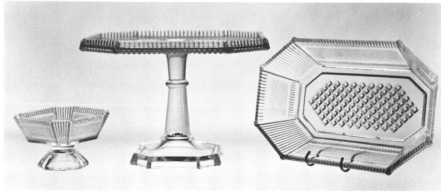

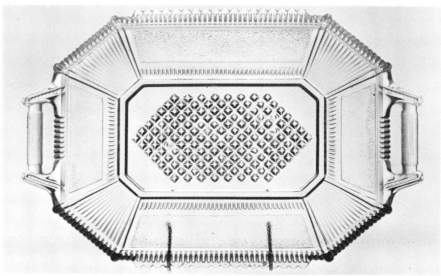

PLEAT
&
PANEL

1. *Comport. ht. 12", square 8".*

2. *Nappy. ht. 2¼", square 3½"*
   Cake Stand. ht. 6", square 8"
   Deep dish. width 5½", length 9"

3. *Bread Platter, length 12½", width 8½".*

4. *Water Pitcher - half gallon ht. 9½"*

5. *Spooner.*

POINTED BULL'S EYE

POINTED
BULL'S EYE

1. *Tumbler ht. 4"*
   Goblet ht. 6¼".
   Pitcher ht. 10¼".

2. *Fruit bowl ht. 2¾", dia.*
   10½".

3. *Nappy ht 2¼", dia. 3¾"*
   Nappy ht. 3¼", dia 5¼"
   Nappy ht. 4½", dia. 7½"

4. *Banana dish - footed ht.*
   9¾"

5. *Covered Comport ht.*
   11", dia. 6½"
   Covered Sugar

6. *Spooner*
   Butter dish

7. *Fruit Bowl fluted ht. 2½",*
   dia. 5½"
   Cream pitcher

167

RAYED HEART

RAYED HEART

1. *Four piece set.*
   Spooner, Covered Butter dish, Covered Sugar, Cream Pitcher.

2. *Nappy. ht. 2", dia. 4"; Nappy. ht. 2", dia. 4".*

Footed Jelly dish. ht. 5½", dia. 5" (pale green to opalescent). Nappy. ht. 2", dia. 4".

3. *Fruit bowl. ht. 3", dia. 8½". Nappy. ht. 2¼", dia. 4".*

RIBBED FORGET-ME-NOT

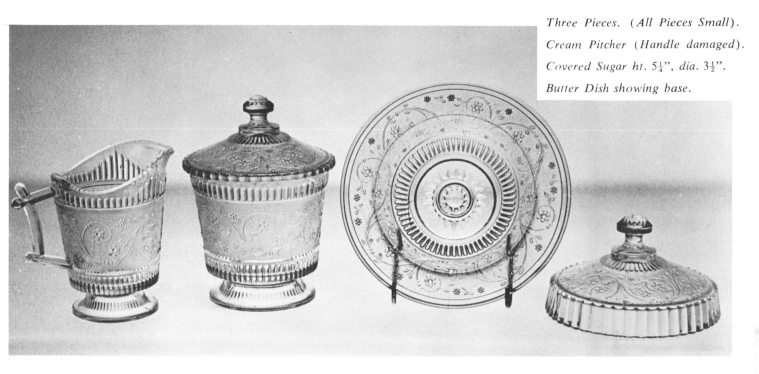

Three Pieces. (All Pieces Small).
Cream Pitcher (Handle damaged).
Covered Sugar ht. 5¼", dia. 3½".
Butter Dish showing base.

PRINCESS FEATHER   LOTUS

Spooner and Covered Sugar.

Spooner and Cream Pitcher.

169

SAWTOOTH

SAWTOOTH

1. *Open Comport. ht.*
   7¾", dia. 8¼".

2. *Open Comport. ht.*
   5½", dia. 8".

3. *Water Pitcher, half*
   gallon. ht. 9½".

4. *Celery footed. ht.*
   9¼", dia. 4½".

Note — full range
of tablewares in-
cluding miniature.

SHELL & TASSEL

SHELL & TASSEL

1. *Sweetmeat basket (blue) in Canadian Silver Plate.*

2. *Glass insert from basket.*

3. *Nappy. Clear. Square 4".*

SHERATON

SHERATON

1. Covered Sugar — note finial similar to Tassel and Crest.
   Spooner
   Cream Pitcher

2. Bread Platter. length 9¾", width 8".
   Footed Nappy. ht. 1¾"; dia. 3½".

Goblet.

3. Milk Pitcher. ht. 7".
   Water Pitcher half gallon. ht. 9".
   Note. This pattern made in full range of tablewares —
   Colours Clear - Amber - Yellow - Green - Light Blue.

STIPPLED SWIRL & STAR

STIPPLED SWIRL & STAR

1. *Butter dish.*
   Cream Pitcher.

2. *Covered Sugar.*

3. *Covered Comport*
   ht. 11", dia. 6¾".

4. *Water Pitcher half*
   gallon ht. 8¾".

5. *Cake Stand. ht. 4½"*
   dia. 9½".

6. *Butter dish showing*
   base.

SQUARE MARSH PINK

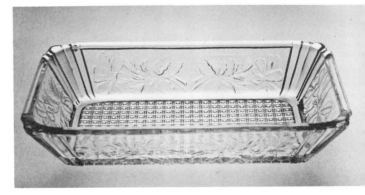

SQUARE MARSH PINK

1. Spooner.

2. Butter dish.

3. Nappy Square 8", ht. 4".

4. Relish dish. width 5", length 8".

Note: This pattern closely resembles Nova Scotia Floral and could be collected as a variant of that pattern — it does come in a complete range of tablewares.

SUNKEN BULL'S EYE

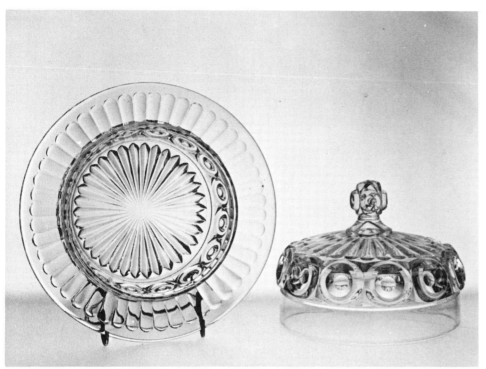

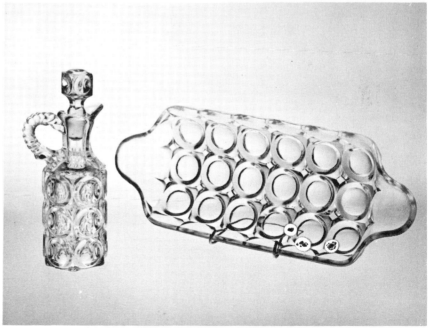

SUNKEN BULL'S EYE

1. *Butter Dish (showing base).*

2. *Spooner. ht. 6".*

3. *Footed Bowl.*

4. *Vinegar Cruet - original stopper. ht. 7¼".*

Pickle Tray or Celery Dish. length 12".

Note: Must be other forms - pitcher - comports, etc. finial and foot can be shown but vinegar handle would not be typical of W/Pitcher or Cream Pitcher.

TOTEM

TOTEM

1. Cream pitcher — Burlington Mark.

2. Butter showing base design which is a repeat of basic pattern.

3. Open Sugar.

4. Open Comport. ht. 8¼", dia. 8¾".

5. Footed bowl fluted. ht. 7½", dia. 9¼".

Note Tumbler shown on another page indicates Water Pitcher made — have not seen goblet.

TRAILWORK

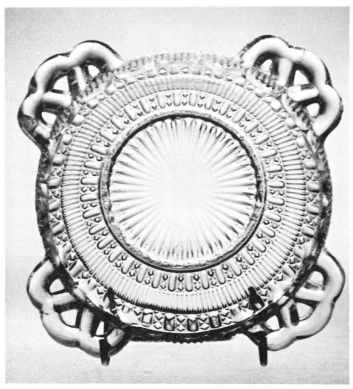

TRAILWORK

1. *Three pieces. Tall footed bowl. ht. 8½" dia. 10".*

   Footed Nappy. ht. 3½", dia. 7¾".

   Cake Stand. ht. 5¾", dia. 9¾".

2. *Plate. dia 8" (blue).*

3. *Cake Stand. (blue). ht. 6¾", dia. 9½".*

   Cake Stand (green). ht. 6", dia. 9½".

4. *Vase clear. ht. 5¼". Vase blue ht. 5".*

WESTWARD HO

WESTWARD HO

1. *Three pieces. Footed Sugar Jar. Footed Butter dish. Footed Cream Pitcher.*

2. *Comport ht. 9", dia. 9", deep 2¾".*

3. *Footed Nappy ht. 2½", dia. 3½"; Footed Nappy ht. 3", dia. 4"; Footed Nappy ht. 3½", dia. 5".*

4. *Covered Comport. ht. 10½", depth 4¾", length 8". Covered Comport. ht 11¼", depth 5¾", length 8¾".*

5. *Bread Platter. width 9", length 13".*

WOODROW

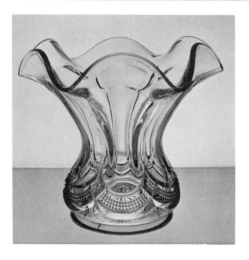

WOODROW

1. *Sherbert. ht 3¼", dia. 4¼" — Pickle. ht. 2½", long 8¾" — Sundae. ht. 6", dia. 3¾". Celery. ht. 6", dia. 4".*
2. *Cake Stand. ht. 6", dia. 9½" — Cake Stand. ht. 6¼", dia. 10½".*
3. *Open Comport. ht. 8", dia. 10¼" — Open Comport. ht. 6", dia. 7½".*
4. *Vase. ht 8", dia 9".*
5. *Four piece set - gold trim. Spooner. Covered Sugar. Butter dish. Creamer.*
   Note. There are at least two versions of the Four piece set completely different in form — gold or ruby trimmed — also clear.
6. *Celery mounted on plate base ht. 7½". Swung vase ht. 11". Syrup Jug ht. 5½".*
7. *Cream Pitcher ht. 4¼". Water Pitcher half gallon ht. 9½".*
8. *Nappy ht. 1½", dia. 4". Bowl ht 3½", dia 9¼". Nappy ht. 2", dia 4¼".*
9. *Pickle dish gold trim ht. 2¼", dia. 5¼". Tumbler ht. 4", dia. 3". Cup ht. 2¼", dia. 3".*

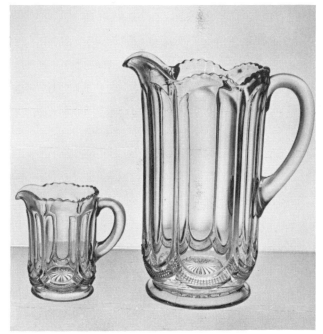

MORE FROM NOVA SCOTIA

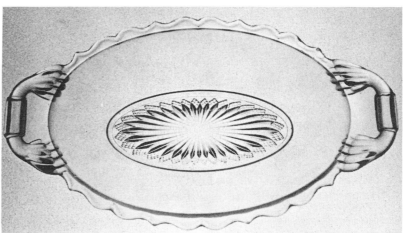

MORE FROM NOVA SCOTIA

1. *Starflower. Footed Bowl.*
2. *Starflower. Straight Sided. Comport.*
3. *Victoria Commemorative Bowl, ht. 7¼", dia. 7".*
4. *Acadian Relish Dish.*

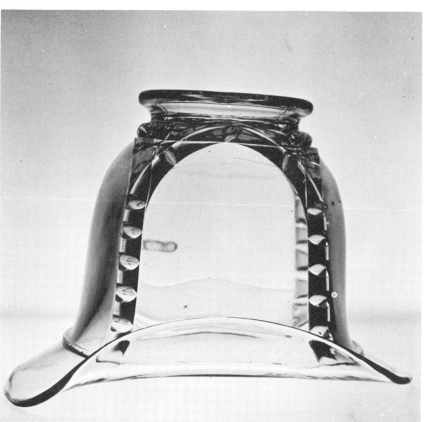

5. *Watch Bell - N.S. Museum. Donated by Mr. G. McKay, N.S.*

6. *Fireman's Hat. Whimsey. (Water Pitcher) donated by Mrs. C. Bransfield, N.S. Museum, ht. approx. 8".*

7. *MacLaren's Cheese Jar.*

8. *Floral Pickle Insert.*

MORE CANADIAN FORMS

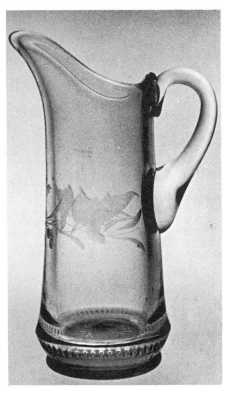

1. *COIN DOT CHEESE BELL* ht. 6½", dia. 8½" - *(delicate pale green shade)*

2. *FOOTED BOWL* - Sheraton ht. 5¼", dia. 7" - *comes in amber and green.*

3. *PLANTER'S PEANUT JAR* - *marked on base "Made in Canada"*

4. *SMALL PITCHER* ht. approx. 6". *Water Pitcher t̶o̶ match seen with BURLINGTON MARK. Pattern similar to AE V Band.*

5. *N.S. DIAMOND BOTTLE* (*stopper fits but is no̶ correct.*

CANE

CANE
Water pitcher half gallon — colours clear blue, green, amber and canary.
Note — comes in full range of tablewares.

RAYED AND OTHER BASES

LATE NUGGET

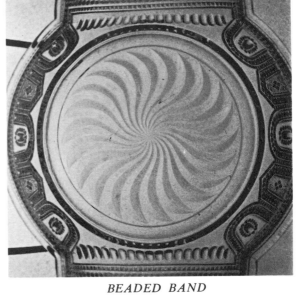

BEADED BAND

N.S. DIAMOND RAY, CROWN and HOBNAIL

101

CANADIAN HORSESHOE

CHANDELIER

AMERICAN PATTERNS
ALSO MADE IN CANADA

The patterns listed are those which have been manufactured in Canada. It is not known whether moulds were purchased in America from mould makers or from the firms direct. It could be that some patterns were manufactured under license. Since documentary evidence proves that many workmen were from the U.S.A. it is likely the moulds were made in the Canadian factories. Moulds could also have been purchased from firms going out of business. Jefferson patterns were manufactured in Toronto from 1912-1925 and also in other Canadian factories.

Adams & Company

    No. 11 THOUSAND EYE   Ca. 1874

Beatty & Sons

        VANDYKE. See **Daisy with V Band.**   Ca. 1885

Belmont Glass Company

    No. 100 DAISY & BUTTON   Ca. 1886

Bryce, McKee & Company

        BEADED OVAL AND SCROLL. Also known
        as **Dot.**   Ca. 1875
        DERBY. See **Pleat & Panel**   Ca. 1882
        DIAMOND SUNBURST   Ca. 1875
        FISH SCALE. Also known as **Coral.**   Ca. 1888
        FILLEY. Also known as **Notched Bull's Eye** Ca. 1875
        IMPERIAL. See **Jacob's Ladder.** Also known
        as **Maltese.**
        NEW YORK. See **Honeycomb.**
        OAKEN BUCKET. See **Old Oaken Bucket**   Ca. 1880
    No. 24 PANELLED FORGET-ME-NOT. Also known
        as **Regal.**   Ca. 1875
        PERT. See **Ribbed Forget-Me-Not**   Ca. 1880
    No. 79 CHAIN WITH STAR   Ca. 1890

Bryce, Higbee & Company

        GRAND. See **Diamond Medallion.**   Ca. 1885
        IDA. See **Sheraton.**   Ca. 1885
        PANELLED THISTLE. See **Canadian Thistle** Ca. 1910

Campbell, Jones & Co.

        ARGYLE. See **Squared Daisy and Diamond** Ca. 1890
        DEWDROP WITH STAR.   Ca. 1877

Canton Glass Co.

        DAHLIA.   Ca. 1885

Doyle & Company

    No. 250 RED BLOCK.   Ca. 1885
        GRAPE AND FESTOON WITH SHIELD   Ca. ?

George Duncan & Sons

        SHELL AND TASSEL   Ca. 1881
        SNAIL.   Ca. 1885
        TREE OF LIFE.   Ca. 1884
        ZIPPERED BLOCK. See **Nova Scotia Ribbon
        and Star.**   Ca. ?

Findlay Flint Glass Co.

    No. 19 FINDLAY   Ca. 1890

RAYED AND OTHER BASES

BEADED OVAL & FAN No. 1

STIPPLED SWIRL & STAR

WOODROW

CONCORDIA MAPLE LEAF

CANADIAN THISTLE

BLOCK

Fostoria Glass Co.

BEADED FLANGE.		Ca. 1891
ROBIN HOOD.		Ca. 1898
VICTOR, known as **Shell and Jewel**. See **Nugget**	Ca. 1900

Gillinder & Sons

LION	Ca. 1876
PIONEER, known as **Westward Ho**	Ca. 1880

A. H. Heisey Glass Co.

IVORINA VERDE.	Ca. 1901

Jefferson Glass Co.

See text.

King Glass Co.

BLEEDING HEART. See **Floral Ware**	Ca. 1875
No. 20 LATTICE.	Ca. 1880
LONDON. Known as **Picket**.	Ca. 1890
No. 198 See **Vine**.	Ca. 1880

The O'Hara Glass Co., Ltd.

No. 82 ANDERSON.	Ca. 1870
CHANDELIER, also known as **Crown Jewels**.	Ca. 1880

Richards & Hartley Flint Glass Co.

LEAF AND DART, also known as Pride.	Ca. 1870
No. 99 MIKADO. See **Daisy** and **Button Cross Bar**	Ca. 1880

Ripley & Company

CLEAR DIAGONAL BAND.	Ca. 1879
MASCOTTE. See **Dominion**	Ca. 1884

CLEAR DIAGONAL BAND

1. *Illustration from Wm. Rogers catalogue.*
2. *Cream Pitcher.*

52 CHURCH STREET, TORONTO.   53

"ELEGANT FLINT GLASS SET."

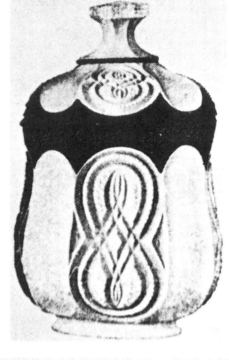

JEFFERSON

1. *Catalogue illustration of Star Line.*

2. *Jefferson No. 254 Pattern. Interlocking Loop.*

3. *Chippendale patent, later acquired by Jefferson Co. Ltd., manufactured at the Toronto Jefferson-Dominion Factory as No. 1600 pattern.*

4. *Jefferson No. 251 Pattern.*

5. *Butter Dish in No. 358 Pattern.*

THE JEFFERSON GLASS COMPANY

Announcement In The August 1912 Issue Of The
"CROCKERY AND GLASS JOURNAL"

"The Jefferson Glass Company, Follansbee, Va; has purchased the glass plant located in Toronto, Canada, formerly conducted under the name of the Independent Producers' Company Limited. The plant there will be known as the Jefferson Glass Company Limited of Toronto, and it will produce the same line of ware that is made at the Follansbee plant together with any additions that are required for the Canadian market. The Toronto plant is a model one in every particular, is practically new and of the best construction — Harry Schnelback will have the management of the Toronto plant . . . Both "Chippendale", tableware and lighting glass-ware lines will be made at the Canadian plant."

Jefferson manufactured attractive and high quality, fluorescent custard ware. These wares are of greenish yellow, or chartreuse, all have brilliance. They also made flint, opaque, green, and blue glass. Some of the glass they produced was over trimmed having gilded rims and finials. Even the imitation cut crystal glass have ruby and gold trim.

Highly decorative lemonade sets and water sets became a fast selling product of this company. Opalescent wares with stripes, polka dots, floral designs and gold trim were featured.

The enamelled sets of coloured glass are desirable collector items particularly the wine or cranberry pitcher with six tumblers. Bride's baskets in Canadian plate with lovely glass bowls can also be found.

In a 1915 catalogue, Jefferson advertised pieces in "Ivorina Verde" Pattern Kamm-Wood Book 2. Page 335, plus some items in a pattern which might be called Ring and Beads. The Jefferson Glass Company opened their Toronto Branch in 1912 but by 1914 the Dominion Glass Company had absorbed them. Gerald Stevens mentions that The Dominion Glass Company was established to prevent the Jefferson Glass Company getting a foothold in Canada and in 1903 obtained the franchise for the Owens Automatic Gathering and Blowing Machine with this very idea in mind. By 1912 when The Jefferson Company did extend operations to Canada, Dominion had consolidated their position and Jefferson's soon became part of Dominion's growing activities. Jefferson continued to produce patterns from the 1880's and 1890's as well as producing known Canadian patterns until 1925. The Canadian Jefferson glass patterns have become highly prized collector pieces. Flint (glass of lead) was also made at the Toronto factory and valued because of being superior "metal". Their No. 275 Ware. RAYED HEART has become the most sought after of all their patterns to date. When collectors realize that many other patterns were made by them in Canada, not only in "flint" but crystal, coloured, opaque ivory, fluorescent, custard and opal glass the choice will widen and prices may level out.

FINIAL, FOOT, HANDLE

FINIAL

RASPBERRY

DAISY with CROSSBAR

RIBBED FORGET-ME-NOT

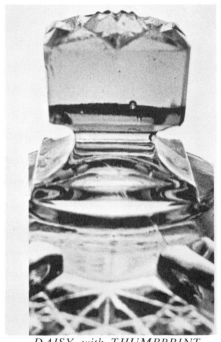

DAISY with THUMBPRINT

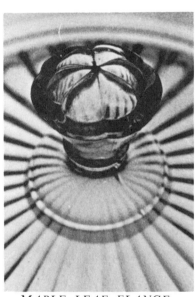

MAPLE LEAF FLANGE

GOOD LUCK

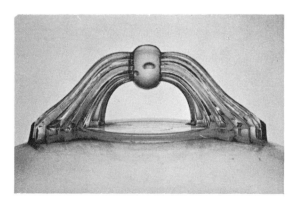

N.S. ACADIA

LION

MINERVA

BUTTONS & BOWS

EARLY NUGGET

DIAMOND RAY

DAISY & "X" BAND

RAYED HEART

STIPPLED SWIRL & STAR

PLEAT & PANEL

FEATHER BAND

194

NS FLORAL

NS RASPBERRY & SHIELD

BEADED BAND

ANDERSON

NS GRAPE & VINE

NS RIBBED BAND

ANDERSON

COLOSSUS

PALMETTE

195

CANADIAN THISTLE

POINTED BULL'S EYE

POINTED BULL'S EYE
VARIANT

N.S. STARFLOWER

N.S. DIAMOND

GREEK KEY & WEDDING RIN

N.S. STARFLOWER

ROUND MARSH PINK
(N.S. Floral)

SQUARE MARSH PINK

LILY OF THE VALLEY

MAPLE LEAF CONCORDIA

MAPLE LEAF ONTARIO

DAISY & DEPRESSED BUTTON

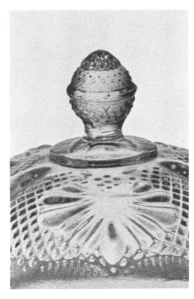

ATHENIAN

No. 204 WARE

CANADIAN

*BEADED OVAL & FAN
No. 1*

TOTEM

197

ESTHER

SUNKEN BULL'S EYE

CHANDELIER

CROSS

RIBBON & STAR

DOMINION

LEAF & DART

BEADED GRAPE

CENTENNIAL

198

CORINTHIAN

AEGIS

GRAPE & FESTOON
WITH SHIELD

THOUSAND EYE

NS VICTORIA
COMMEMORATIVE

JACOB'S LADDER

101

PRINCESS FEATHER

SHERATON

LOOP & PILLAR

BEAD & PETAL

BEAD & PETAL

LILY-OF-THE-VALLEY

WOODROW

BEADED ARCH

PRINCESS FEATHER

DEER & DOG

FROSTED FLOWER BAND

COLONIAL

COLONIAL

COLONIAL

COLONIAL

BLOCK VARIANT

PANELLED FORGET-ME-NOT

PICKET

FLOWER & QUILL

NOTE: Finials, like Handles and Foot, vary from absolute simplicity to extremely ornate. Colonial Pattern has at least five different Finials. Nova Scotia Glass Works used the same Finials on several patterns and sometimes two different Finials on one pattern.

FOOT

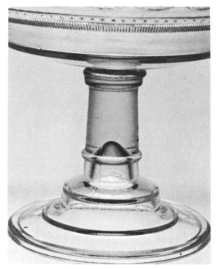

SHERATON

ATHENIAN

DIAMOND MEDALLION

N S RIBBED BAND

BEADED BAND

COLOSSUS

SAWTOOTH

RIBBED FORGET-ME-NOT

FISHSCALE

DIAMOND MEDALLION

NS STAR FLOWER

NS STAR FLOWER

CORINTHIAN

CORINTHIAN

GOOD LUCK

GOOD LUCK

DEER & DOG

DEER & DOG

LATE NUGGET

MAPLE LEAF ONTARIO

ATHENIAN

TOTEM

JACOB'S LADDER

CANADIAN DRAPE

101

PALMETTE

SAWTOOTH

PICKET

BEADED GRAPE

BEADED OVAL

PLEAT and PANEL

TRAILWORK

SUNKEN BULL'S EYE

ANDERSON

ACADIAN

NS DIAMOND RAY

BEADED OVAL & FAN No. 2

DAISY WITH X BAND

DAISY
WITH DEPRESSED BUTTON

DAISY WITH CROSS BAR

POINTED BULL'S EYE

ESTHER

NS DIAMOND

LATTICE

STIPPLE SWIRL & STAR

HANDLES

CRANBERRY
COIN DOT W/P

BLOCK W/P

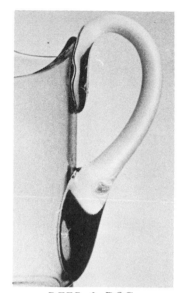

DEER & DOG
CREAM PITCHER

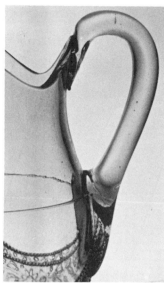

CANADIAN DRAPE
W/P

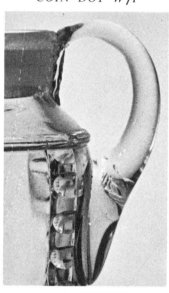

N.S. CROWN
SYRUP

N.S. CROWN
CREAM PITCHER

SAWTOOTH W/P

101 W/P

JACOB'S LADDER
W/P

LILY-OF-THE-VALLEY
W/P

PALMETTE W/P

POINTED BULL'S EYE
W/P

207

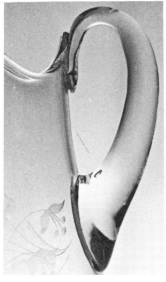

ETCHED W/P

HONEY COMB W/P

GRAPE & FESTOON
with SHIELD

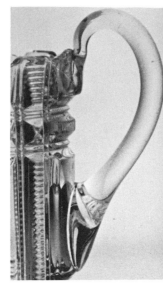

N.S. RIBBON & STAR
W/P

TOTEM CREAM PITCHER

DAISY
CREAM PITCHER

DAISY W/P

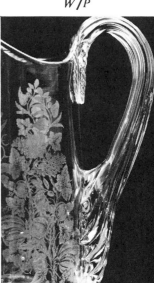

ETCHED W/P

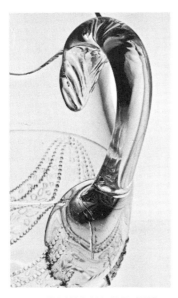

CANADIAN DRAPE
CREAM PITCHER

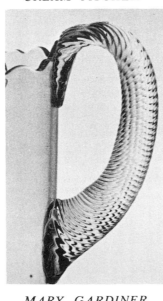

MARY GARDINER
W/P

WOODROW W/P

BEAD & PETAL
CREAM PITCHER

208

BEADED GRAPE W/P

DIAMOND MEDALLION W/P

EARLY NUGGET W/P

LATE NUGGET W/P

BEADED OVAL & FAN No. 1 - W/P

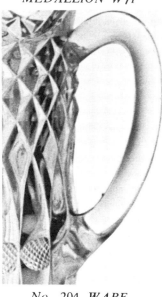

No. 204 WARE W/P

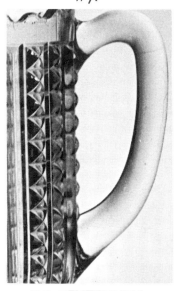

N.S. CENTENNIAL

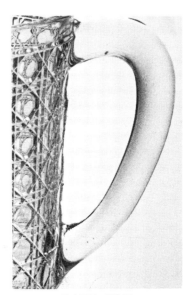

CANE W/P

BEADED OVAL WINDOW W/P

MAPLE LEAF W/P

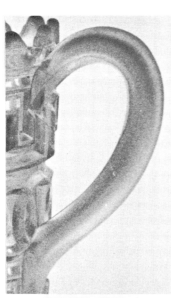

GREEK KEY & WEDDING RING W/P

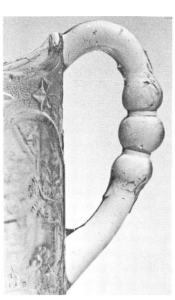

CANADIAN W/P

209

N.S. VICTORIA
COMMEMORATIVE
CREAMER

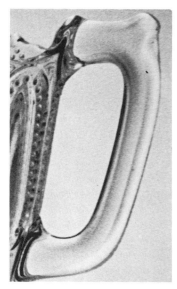

101 CREAMER

N.S. DIAMOND RAY
W/P

SHERATON
MILK PITCHER

ATHENIAN W/P

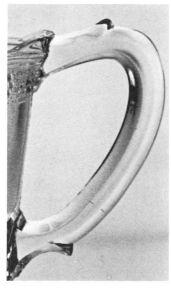

N.S. RASPBERRY
& SHIELD W/P

N.S. GRAPE & VINE
CREAMER

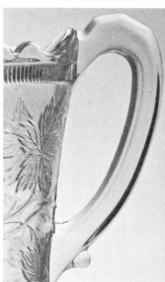

N.S. GRAPE & VINE
W/P

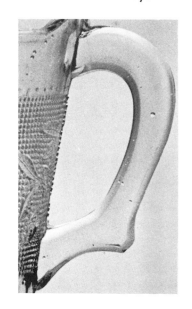

DAHLIA W/P

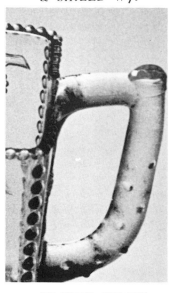

BEADED GRAPE
CREAMER

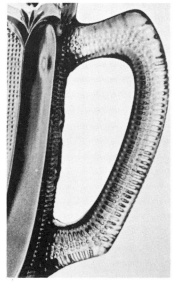

STIPPLED SWIRL
& STAR W/P

LOTUS
CREAMER

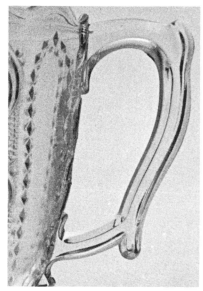

COLOSSUS W/P

BEADED ARCH CREAMER

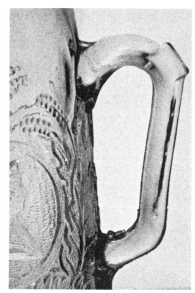

VICTORIA W/P

DAHLIA W/P

FROSTED FLOWER BAND W/P

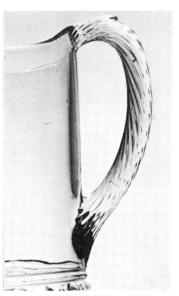

CHANDELIER W/P

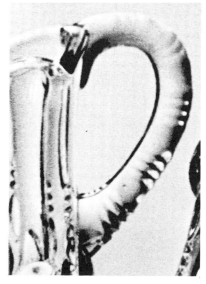

LOOP & PILLAR CREAMER

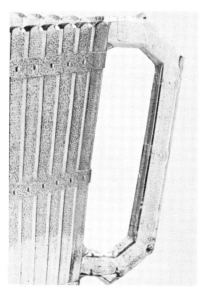

PICKET W/P

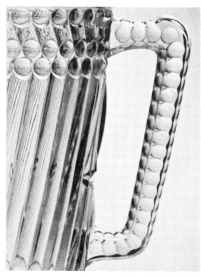

BUTTON & BOWS W/P

LOTUS CREAMER

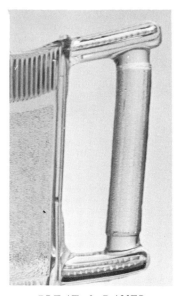

PLEAT & PANEL
W/P

GOOD LUCK W/P

DAISY & DEPRESSED
BUTTON W/P

DAISY & CROSS BAR
W/P

RIBBED-FORGET-ME-
NOT - CREAMER

MINERVA W/P

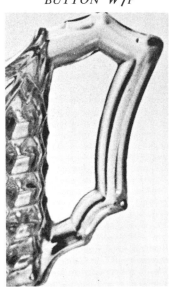

JACOB'S LADDER
CREAMER

COLONIAL SYRUP

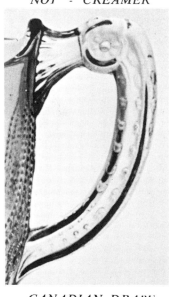

CANADIAN DRAPE
CREAMER

BEADED OVAL
& FAN - W/P

CROSS
CREAMER

212

GOBLETS

BEAVER BAND

BEAVER BAND (Script)

BLOCK

WESTWARD HO BUFFALO

WESTWARD HO DEER

RED BLOCK

213

NS TANDEM

N S RASPBERRY & SHIELD

NS RASPBERRY

LILY OF THE VALLEY

DIAMOND SUNBURST

NS DIAMOND

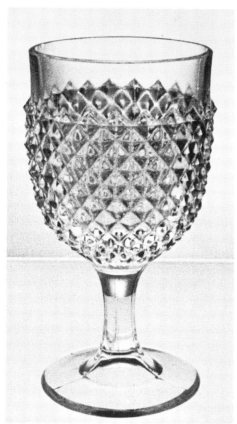

DIAMOND   SAWTOOTH   CANADIAN DRAPE

NS RIBBON & STAR   MAPLE LEAF   MAPLE LEAF (on tree stem)

BUTTON ARCHES

DAISY WITH
DEPRESSED BUTTON

CANE

KENLEE

HONEY COMB CORDIAL

CAPE COD

BUCKLE

BEADED ARCH

AEGIS

101

GOTHIC

COLOSSUS

N.S. FLORAL

DIAMOND MEDALLION

CHAIN WITH STAR

LOTUS

SHERATON

CANADIAN

PLEAT & PANEL

CROSS OR MIKADO FAN

CANADIAN THISTLE (*Green*)

PALMETTE

FEATHER BAND

GRADUATED DIAMOND

219

PANELLED
FORGET - ME - NOT

MINERVA

GOOD LUCK

ODD FELLOW

DOMINION

BEADED GRAPE

PINEAPPLE BAND
(American)

THOUSAND EYE BAND

DAISY
WITH PETTICOAT BAND

CHANDELIER

BEADED BAND

LION

221

DAHLIA　　　　　　NOVA SCOTIA CROWN　　　　　THOUSAND EYE

ST. JOHN'S ETCHED SPRAY　　　ST. JOHN'S ETCHED BAND　　　ESTHER

WOODROW

WOODROW
WITH RUBY FLASH

CROSS or BOLING

BEADED OVAL & FAN No. 2

RAYED HEART

RAYED HEART (Showing Base

DAISY WITH CROSSBAR

LATTICE

BLOCK & FAN

THOUSAND EYE THREE PANEL

JACOB'S LADDER

COLONIAL

CANADIAN GLASS IN COLOUR

1. *Opal glass lamp in the Canadian Heart pattern (deep-blue) Burlington Glass Works.*

2. *Opal glass lamp in the Princess Feather pattern. (pale blue) Burlington Glass Works.*

3. *No. 102 — Bull's Eye Lamp, popular in mixed and/or matched techniques, deep blue foot, clear font. Burlington Glass Works.*

4. *No. 102, Bull's Eye Lamp, different shade of blue. These lamps were made in a variety of colours and combinations of colours as well as clear and coloured. Burlington Glass Works.*

5. *Clear glass lamp with Chevron foot and amber font. Burlington Glass Works.*

6. *Lamp with white opalescent Coin Dot font. Burlington Glass Works.*

7. *Guardian Angel Lamp, 1877-1905, attributed to Excelsior Glass Co., St. Johns. Shards found at Burling Glass Site indicate that the lamps were also manfactured there.*

8. *Opal lamp in Shell pattern, delicate shadings. Salt shakers also made in this pattern. Burlington Glass Works.*

9. *Beaver Sealer with the beaver facing left, this sealer is much heavier and darker in colour than the amber sealers with beaver facing right.*

10. *Cranberry salt and pepper shakers in Canadian silver plate.*

11. *Mould-blown opal Lamp 'Fern' pattern. (blue).*

12. *Mould blown Opal, hand-painted shakers. Burlington Glass Works.*

13. *No. 102. Bull's Eye Lamp. Clear green glass.*

14. *Salt and pepper shakers in glass stand matching design and colour of No. 102 lamp.*

15. *Apple Blossom lamp, this pattern was also used for full range of table wares. Burlington Glass Works.*

16. *Cosmos pattern lamp, also made in full range of table wares. Burlington Glass Works.*

1	2	3	4
5	6	7	8
9	10	11	12
13	14	15	16

Key to Coloured Glass.
Plate No. 3

BEAVER AND MAPLE LEAF
BRACKET LAMP

BURLINGTON
ART GLASS LAMP

DARK BLUE FOOT
CLEAR FONT

A VARIETY TRIO

GREEN & YELLOW
CANADIAN HEART LAMPS

BEAVER HANGING LAMP

ART GLASS LAMPS
BURLINGTON

GREEK KEY LAMP

CANADIAN LAMPS

1. BURLINGTON — BULL'S EYE LAMPS.

   Six sizes shown - clear "flint" non-lead glass.

2. BURLINGTON - FEATHER DUSTER font and CHEVRON base design - clear "flint" non-lead glass.

3. See No. 1

4. BURLINGTON - FAN clear "flint" non-lead glass.

5. BURLINGTON - CROSS hand lamp - clear "flint" non-lead glass.

6. BURLINGTON - CANADIAN DRAPE base - plain font - clear "flint" non-lead glass.

CANADIAN DRAPE

BEADED LATTICE AND FRAME

1. CROSS BASE - CHEVRON POST - CLEAR FONT   3. No. 101 LAMP.
2. CROSS FONT - CHEVRON POST - PANELLED BASE

PRINCESS FEATHER
Lamp with Handle

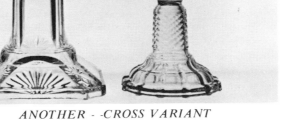

No. 101 LAMP   ANOTHER --CROSS VARIANT   JEFFERSON TABLE LAMP
No. 101 LAMP

FOUR NUTMEG LAMPS
Made in Montreal. In clear, coloured, milk and opalescent metal handles.

FOUR GUARDIAN ANGEL LAMPS

Four small coloured hand-lamps, two bearing the lettering on the outside "L" Ange Gardien-Extra-C. H. Binks, and Co. Montreal, and the others plain.

Clear Guardian Angel Lamp with Nutmeg Chimney

The "Guardian Angel" lamps come in various colours and clear glass; they are of different small sizes and shapes and some are even more "bilingual" than those pictured, having "Guardian Angel" printed in French and English. All have applied handles, some finished at the bottom with a flourish or "Trail", and all are rare.

The globes or shades and the metal fittings are interchangeable, and cannot be identified.

The other lamps in the picture are so precisely identical in every measurement, even when gauged with calipers, that one would say it must have come from the same mould were it not that "Angel" mould bore lettering. However, there is one difference between the four; whereas the "angel" lamps show distinct marks of the two-piece mould into which the glass was blown, the plain lamps have been turned in the mould so that no mould marks show. Can it be that this was done to eradicate the lettering as well as the mould marks?

This conjecture is encouraged by the fact that there are very faint lines or scorings around the bowl just where the printing would have been.

Binks & Co. operated in Montreal as importers from 1877 to 1905. Although Binks and the church supply houses were within a few blocks of the Montreal office and warehouse of the Excelsior Glass Co. (whose plant at St. John's, incidentally, was near the village of L'ange Gardien) Mr. Stevens found from excavation of shards that at least some clear glass lamps bearing this lettering were made in Hamilton, Ontario. Information from "A Guide To Early Canadian Glass" by Hilda & Kevin Spence.

229

LAMP BURNERS, MADE IN CANADA

Climax Slip Burner

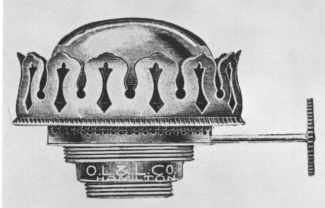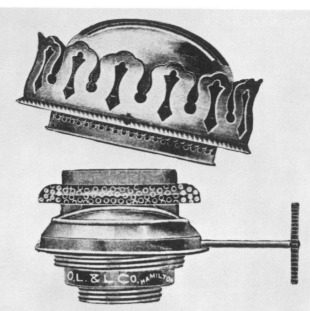

D or No. 3 Climax Slip Burner fits No. 2 and No. 3 collar; takes D wick.

Our D or No. 3 Climax Slip Burner has removable Gallery.

Packed 20 dozen in a case
Weight, 70 lbs.

"D" Banner Burner

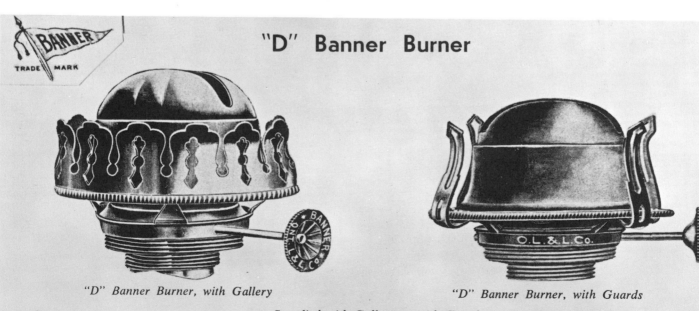

"D" Banner Burner, with Gallery

"D" Banner Burner, with Guards

Supplied with Gallery or with Guards
Fits either B or D collar; takes D wick
This Burner gives a large white flame, and is admirably adapted for parlor and hanging lamps.

Packed 20 dozen in a case.
Weight, 70 lbs.

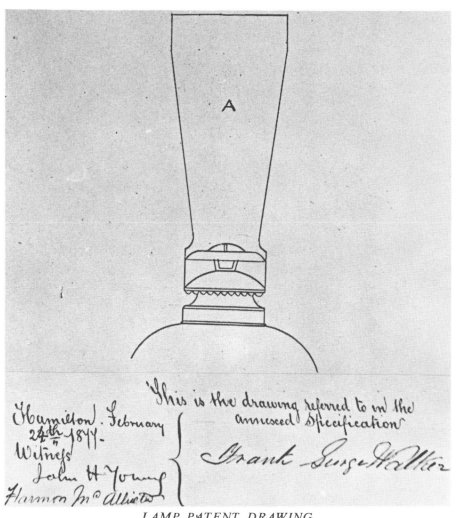

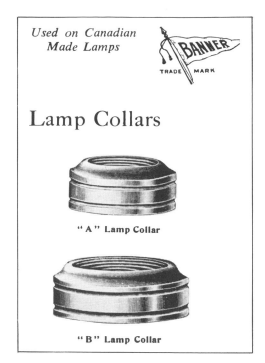

Used on Canadian Made Lamps

Lamp Collars

"A" Lamp Collar

"B" Lamp Collar

LAMP PATENT DRAWING
George Walker of Hamilton - February 24th, 1877

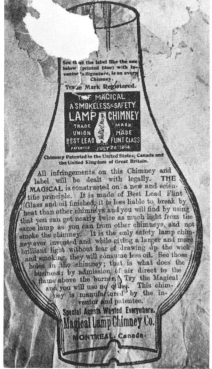

LAMP CHIMNEY
Dominion Glass Co. Ltd.

CANADIAN DESIGN Trade Mark Registered July 26th, 1894

RUBBINGS *by Betty Milligan*

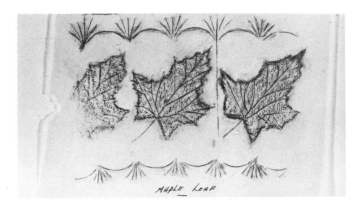

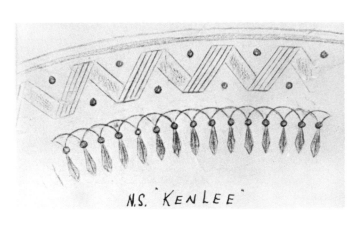

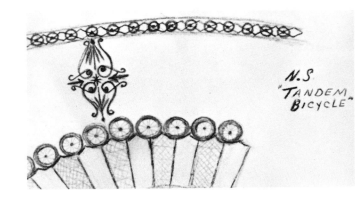

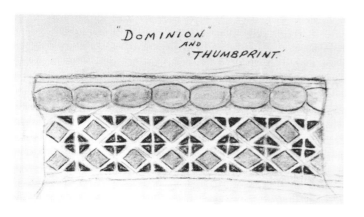

"DOMINION" AND "THUMBPRINT"

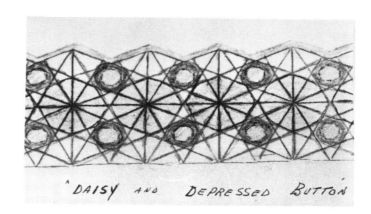

"DAISY AND DEPRESSED BUTTON"

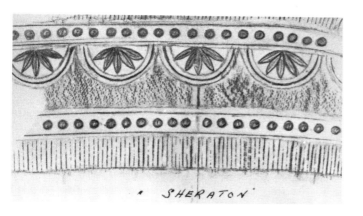

"SHERATON"

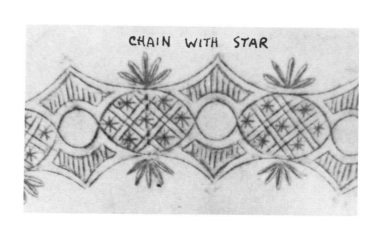

CHAIN WITH STAR

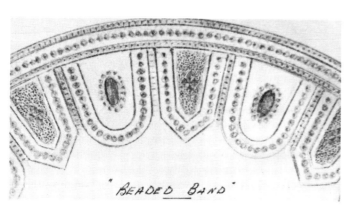

"BEADED BAND"

LATTICE

DIAMOND MEDALLION

No. 101 LAMP

1875-1915

233

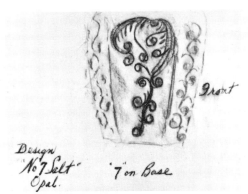

HOW TO MAKE A RUBBING

Over the years of collecting, I have found that to make a rubbing of each new pattern I have obtained a very convenient method of recording Canadian Glass. They could be used and easily carried in purse or glove compartment of your car when antiquing. This eliminates the necessity of carrying a valuable piece which could be easily broken. Also it is possible to make a tracing with permission of an item, not yet in your collection, for future reference.

ARTICLES OF GLASS FOR RUBBINGS: Anything with a pattern — fruit jar (light inside), lamp base (light under), lamp font, insulators, bottles, etc. Some patterns are easily rubbed such as Floral, Tandem, Bicycle, Tassel and Crest because they are the finer detailed. Other patterns such as Bullseye, Chandelier and Saw-tooth are more difficult because they are heavy and deep and tear the paper. It is possible to trace or outline the latter group over a strong light.

MATERIALS NEEDED: Paper, Red Pencil, Scotch Tape, Strong Moveable Light, and Outdoor Christmas Lights.

PAPER: I have tried Onion Skin, but I prefer tracing paper. example "The Studio Tracing Pad" — green tinted — a Hilroy product.

PENCIL: Red — little wax as possible — I prefer "Eagle Verithin" Carmine Red 745.

LIGHT: Goose neck desk lamp with a very strong bulb. This is positioned close to article to be rubbed. Outdoor Christmas lights could be used inside or under the article to be rubbed for better lighting of the pattern. e.g. fruit jar.

PREPARATION: 1) Tape edge of paper to anchor it, perhaps in four places. The tape may be left on the tracing paper, when rubbing is completed, and the over hang cut off. The paper should be only large enough to catch one complete outline of the pattern.

2) Press pattern with finger to form the outline.

3) With SIDE of lead rub lightly, find the best direction to rub (horizontally, vertically, or diagonally) and then press a little firmer until red outline catches all details. It is not necessary to erase unwanted light pencil rubbing as the pattern outline should be heavily defined.

4) Remove tape carefully — and — Voila — Beautiful

Some patterns seem difficult, but with patience and practice they can be lovely when finished. Copies of rubbings are easily made on most copying machines.

If you "think glass", perhaps you would like to frame some for pictures in old pine framing. Try outlining in black ink or fill in the background with soft colours.

Betty Milligan

THE ROBERT BUDDO BOTTLES

On the 22nd day of October, 1913, Robert Buddo registered an industrial design of an ink bottle, being a comic representation of a woman, on the same day he registered a second design, the mate to the first, a comic representation of a man.

On January 6th, 1914, Charles H. Henkels of Philadelphia, Pennsylvania, patented his design for the Carter's Ink Company of Boston, Massachusetts. The designs which represented the figure of a woman (Mrs. Carter) and a man (Mr. Carter) were identical to the figures registered by Robert Buddo, resident of Westmount, in the Province of Quebec and Dominion of Canada.

Albert Christian Revi, **American Pressed Glass and Figure Bottles**, page 363, gives the story of the success of these bottles when used in a National advertising campaign between 1914 and 1916. A coupon and twenty-five cents brought the sender a pair of these comic little bottles. Revi says some 50,000 coupons returned gave adequate proof.

Whilst the evidence shows that this is actually a Canadian design the question remains, were any of these bottles ever made in Canada? The first of the bottles sent out by Carters were made in Germany of pottery and painted in bright colours. After World War I started they found an American source and the bottles looked similar but for the "Made in Germany" which was on the earlier supplies. Later the bottles were made in glass.

I Robert Buddo, of Westmount, in the Province of
Quebec and Dominion of Canada, hereby request you to register in
the name of Robert Buddo an Industrial Design of an Ink Bottle
of which I am the proprietor. I declare that the said Industrial
Design was not in use to my knowledge by any other person than
myself at the time of my adoption thereof. The said Industrial
Design consists of the comic representation of a woman.

A drawing of the said Industrial Design is hereunto
annexed.

Signed at *Montreal*
this 22 day of *Octr* A. D. 1913, in the presence of the
two undersigned witnesses.

Robert Buddo

Witnesses:

E. H. B. Dixon
J. H. Dyson

The Minister of Agriculture,
Ottawa, Canada.

I, Robert Buddo, of Westmount, in the Province of Quebec and Dominion of Canada, hereby request you to register in the name of Robert Buddo an Industrial Design of an Ink Bottle of which I am the proprietor. I declare that the said Industrial Design was not in use to my knowledge by any other person than myself at the time of my adoption thereof. The said Industrial Design consists of the comic representation of a man.

A drawing of the said Industrial Design is hereunto annexed.

Signed at *Montreal* this *22* day of *Octr* A. D. 1913, in the presence of the two undersigned witnesses.

Robert Buddo

Witnesses:

E. H. B. Dixon

J. H. Dyson

The Minister of Agriculture,
        Ottawa, Canada.

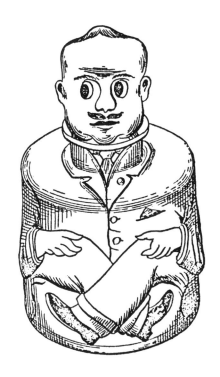

CANADIAN MADE BOTTLES

1. Raspberry Vinegar Maple Leaf Bottle.
2. Reverse of Raspberry Vinegar.
3. Citrate of Magnesia attributed Diamond Glass Co.
4. Beaver Bottle - Beaver looking right. Barrie.

5. Beaver Bottle - Beaver looking left. Toronto.
6. Reverse of Beaver bottle.
7. Raspberry Syrup Bottle.

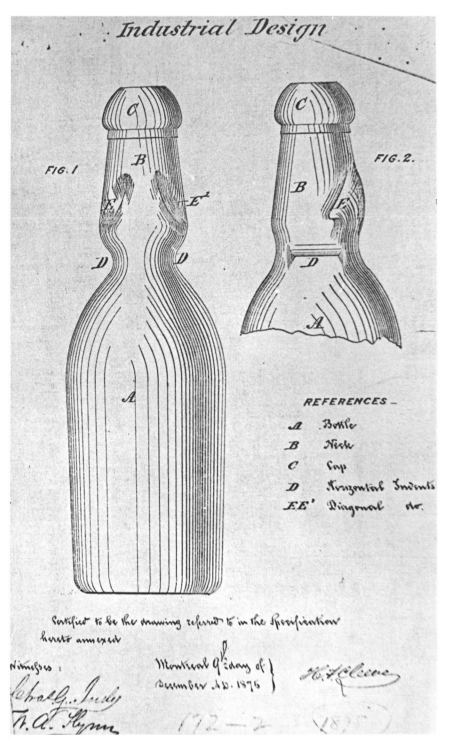

BOTTLES

1. *Patent drawing showing 1876 as date of Candian design for pinch neck bottle.*
2. *Bottle made in Manchester, England for N.S. firm.*
3. *Trenton flask on display at Nova Scotia Museum.*
4. *Liniment bottle Douglas Egyptian Liniment Co., was operated by Willett Dollar in the late 1800's and continued by his son and daughter-in-law, Doug and Marjory Dollar, then went out of business. (Napanee).*

THREE PHARMACIST'S BOTTLES

THREE MILK GLASS CONTAINERS

HISTORY AND DATA OF CANADIAN SEALERS

(Condensed from NORTH AMERICAN FRUIT JAR INDEX, courtesy Marion & Douglas Bird)

THE ACME SEAL

Made at the Manitoba Glass Manufacturing Company, Beausejour, Manitoba (1907-1914). A shard was found on the site, see Max Provick, **Beausejour's Glass Works,** Canadian (antiques) Collector, January, 1967.

BEAVER

Beaver jars manufactured at the Ontario Glass Company, Kingsville, Ontario (1899-1902). John Sheeler dug up the Beaver pieces at the site. Now at the Canadian Gallery in Toronto. The Beaver Jar was not made by the Beaver Flint Glass Company (Toronto, Ontario, 1897-1948). This firm was a secondary manufacturer, making tubes, vials, etc., from glass tubing supplied by primary manufacturers. The pint size is by far the scarcest.

BEAVER FACING LEFT

Pale aqua pints and amber pints. The ground lip would be of pre-1902 manufacture, and possibly by Dominion's predecessor, Diamond Glass Co. (1890-1902).

CORONA JAR

Made in Canada by Consumers Glass Company. The "C" within an equilateral triange on the bottom is the trademark. Later, the three corners of the triangle were rounded.

THE DOOLITTLE

Manufactured at Wallaceburg, Ontario, by the Sydenham Glass Co. in 1901. It has a very unusual closure, the glass lid carrying two metal "ears", that swing around and hook over the neck. Dominion Glass Company manufactured a jar with a lightening fastener in 1915. It is embossed ERIE-LIGHTENING. Their catalogues show this only in the quart size, the pint and half-gallon sizes being plain. However, there is an earlier ERIE, manufactured at the Erie Glass Works, Port Colborne, Ontario (1895-1899). Not much is known of this firm's output. They made a pickle jar with the word ERIE on the bottom, and a picnic flask with the same marking. Their fruit jars embossed ERIE-E (framed in hexagon) FRUIT JAR. The word ERIE on the bottom, and a ground lip. Its glass lid has a large E in a hexagon.

THE EGCO IMPERIAL

Made by the Excelsior Glass Co. (St. Johns, Quebec 1878-1880; Montreal, Quebec, 1880-1883). It takes a plain glass lid. The Excelsior Glass Company manufactured a glass lid with their name, but color and scarcity indicate that this was for another jar, not yet known.

EXCELSIOR GLASS CO. REGISTERED APR. 1879

Mark on above mentioned lid.

CANADIAN SEALERS

WALLACEBURG
"DOOLITTLE" - Patented Dec. 3, 1901

THE AMERICAN QUART
PORCELAIN LINED

ANCHOR PINT

ANCHOR QUART

EXCELSIOR GLASS CO. INCORPORATED 1879

Since the American firm, EXCELSIOR GLASS WORKS ran from 1863 to 1886, there can be no confusion. The date usually given for the incorporation of EXCELSIOR IN CANADA 1878. However, their lid shows that the actual incorporation went through in 1879.

THE GEM RUTHERFORDS

Made by Hamilton Glass Works during the period of the Rutherford ownership (starting in 1872).

PERFECT SEALS

Made in 1915 by Dominion Glass Company. The STAR is a very rare jar, coming in three sizes, pint, quart and half-gallon. In shape, shape of bottom, mold markings, colour, it exactly resembles the BEAVER. The possibility that it could have been made by Ontario Glass Manufacturing Company is being considered.

CROWNS

Crowns manufactured from 1929 on have the date on the bottom, and are made by Dominion Glass Company. Occasionally the date is missing on the bottom. AQUA CROWNS with smooth lips manufactured 1902 and 1928 inclusive, if there is no date on the bottom. A few of these jars have HD4, HD5, 4DH on the bottom. This means Hamilton Works of the Dominion Glass Company, and it is thought that 4 stands for 1924, and so on, although it has never been established that it does not stand for 1914. CROWN EMBLEM appears on a pint manufactured in 1915 by Dominion. In that year they made a quart and a half gallon with CROWN emblems. (These are shown in one of their catalogues). CROWN EMBLEM appears in a 1924 canning booklet put out by Dominion Glass Co. CROWN EMBLEM also appears in 1902 Eaton's Catalogue. A NEW CROWN EMBLEM (in the heart-shaped series). The half gallon is now known to have been made in 1880. It is very likely that all the heart-shaped crown emblems date about 1880. THE CROWNS with no dots are thought to have been manufactured by Hamilton Glass Works very shortly after 1867. Hamilton started off in 1865 with closures of the type found in the 1861 Millvilles. The no-dot crown is attributed to Hamilton by glass collectors because the mold-markings, the shape of the jar, and the base shape exactly resemble the GEM RUTHER FORDS, which are known to have been made at Hamilton. It is thought that the crown emblem was originally used on pottery to indicate Imperial measure.

THE DEXTER

The Dexter has a mouth part-way between a small-mouth pint, and a regular pint, exactly resembling the mouth of the certain GEM RUTHERFORDS, and would therefore be of Hamilton manufacture. (Geo. Rutherford and Company were the owners of Hamilton Glass Works in 1872. From 1865 to 1871, Gachell, Moore and Company were the owners.)

GEM

GEM (script), NEW GEM (script), 1908, GEM (script), Wallaceburg, GEM (script) are so very similar in design and glass that they can all be attributed to the Wallaceburg plant of Sydenham Glass Co. (later the Dominion Glass Co., Wallaceburg plant).

THE GREEK KEY DESIGN JAR

Manufactured by Burlington Glass Co. See Royal Ontario Museum leaflet.

CANADIAN SEALERS

BEAVER *Crosshatch Tail*
American one-half gallon

AMBER BEAVER
facing left (rare)

BEAVER *Stipple tail*
Imperial one-half gallon

BEE HIVE
One-half gallon

BEST
One quart

THE BURLINGTON
B.G. Co. Quart
Note mismarked B.C. Go.

CANADIAN SEALERS

BURLINGTON QUART
1880

CORONET
One half gallon

CROWN
No Dot

RING WITH CROWN
No Word - gallon

CROWN
Word on - one half gallon

CROWN
Bulge quart

245

CANADIAN SEALERS

CROWN
Tall, Narrow

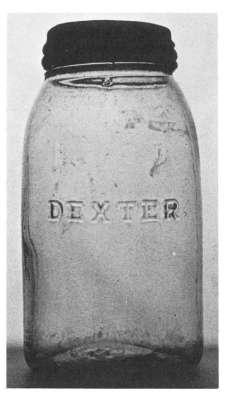

DEXTER
Quart

DIAMOND
D.G. Co., One-half gallon

THE GEM
Rutherford & Co.
Hamilton Glass Co.

THE SAME
Embossing Different

GEM
H.F.C. on Wings of Cross

CANADIAN SEALERS

IDEAL IMPERIAL
Quart

HAMILTON GLASSWORKS
One quart

HAMILTON GLASSWORKS
No. 2

HAMILTON GLASSWORKS
No. 4
Has whittle marks
due to cold mould

HAMILTON GLASSWORKS
One-half gallon

STAR
One quart

CANADIAN SEALERS

THE EGGO
Imperial Quart

THE ROSE

TRUE FRUIT
J. H. S. Co.

GREEK KEY
One-half gallon

THE POINTS TO NOTE
WHEN COLLECTING SEALERS

FACTOR	POSITIVE QUALITIES	NEGATIVE QUALITIES
Embossing	prominent and distinct	worn looking
Closure	Complete, proper, matching closure	No closure Incorrect closure Partial closure
Condition	No damage	Lip chips, cracks in lip, stain
Color	Attractive color	Less attractive
Glass	Whittled, bubbly	Machine-like
Metal closure	Old but no damage	Rusty, corroded
Screw band	Tightens properly	Threads stripped

See Bird, North American Fruit Jar Index

CANADIAN GLASS IN COLOUR

1. *Free-blown, aquamarine-coloured pitcher with lily-pads from the Mallory Glass Works. On display at the Sigmund Samuel Canadiana Gallery, Royal Ontario Museum.*

2. *"Lilies" or cornucopia, blue and amethyst, factory source not known. Amber and green 'Lilies' were made at the Foster Glass Works, Port Colborne (1895-1899) see Stevens, Canadian Glass, 1825/1925, page 35.*

3. *Cranberry glass pickle insert, oil enamel hand painted decoration. Stand Canadian Silver Plate.*

4. *Carafe, water pitcher and syrup jug in shades of pink with white. Burlington Glass Works.*

5. *Paperweight made for T. Bassett. On display at the Sigmund Samuel Canadiana Gallery. Royal Ontario Museum.*

6. *Paperweight. Masonic Emblem. Also on display at Royal Ontario Museum.*

7. *Milk Glass. Crown covered sugar and cream pitcher, painted on the scroll like elements. See Millard, Opal Glass, plate 214. Burlington Glass Works.*

8. *Beaded Oval Window goblet. (pale yellow) Burlington Glass Works.*

9. *Opalescent Fern leaf, white with clear handle and stopper. Oil or vinegar cruet.*

10. *Trail work, cake stands, pale blue and pale green. Factory source not known.*

11. *Tankard-type pitcher, bronze and red colourings flecked with gold. Burlington Glass Works.*

12. *Milk Glass covered sugar (two handles) and cream pitcher. Burlington Glass Works.*

13. *Rayed Heart footed jelly, shading from pale green to opalescent. (rare). Jefferson-Dominion, Toronto.*

14. *White Coin Dot Pitcher. Burlington Glass Works.*

15. *Whimseys in deep blue glass, Swan and Pig. On display at Royal Ontario Museum.*

16. *Opalescent white and clear lemon 'Lattice' pitcher. Burlington Glass Works.*

1	2	3	4
5	6	7	8
9	10	11	12
13	14	15	16

Key to Coloured Glass.
Plate. No. 4

THE BURLINGTON MARK

Many articles made at the Burlington factory requiring hand applied handles have been noted bearing a distinguishing mark which does not appear to have been used at any other factory.

Kamm-Wood **Book One** refers to this mark on page 195. Describing the applied handle on a **Deer and Dog Pitcher,** she says "the top is turned under with a tab stamped with seven V's". Also mentioned is the fact that the handle is corrugated down its entire length. Kamm compares it to the pattern **Centennial,** page 129. John R. Sheeler describes it as consisting of a series of fan-like marks which resemble a "shell".

This mark has been found on **Coin Dot water pitchers, opal 'Lattice' and 'Snail' pattern syrup jugs, Block, Garfield (Canadian) Drape, '101', Esther, Totem, Chain with Star, Mary Gardiner Type, Lion, Cosmos, Daisy and Depressed Button, "Robin Hood", Diamond with Sunburst, Swirl, Bulbous Bull's Eye, Pillow Encircled, Block Band, AE.V Band, and Marsh Fern pitchers.** Also on a variety of etched pitchers, tankards, jugs and art glass pieces.

It is interesting to note that the Burlington Mark is not found only on pitchers and syrup jugs. The authors recently discovered that it was on the uppermost point of a Jack-in-the-pulpit vase on the inside of the flower. Also discovered two baskets with the mark on the handles where they were attached to the basket. It was used on quality pattern glass and opalescent glass. Whilst it cannot be taken as definite proof that articles bearing this mark were made only at Burlington there is at this time no evidence that it was in use elsewhere. Further research will, we believe, point up the origin and provide information about the handle-appliers who used what must have been a specially designed tool.

BURLINGTON MARK

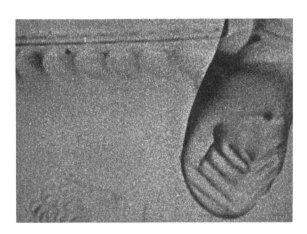

1. Snail vinegar cruet. 2. Lion water pitcher. 3. Robin Hood syrup jug. 4. Cranberry Coin Dot Water pitcher.
5. Close-up of mark on basal tab of water pitcher.

There are several patterns in the Kamm-Wood Enciclodpedia of American Glass which are mentioned as having a mark of like nature, since the maker or place of origin was not known to Mrs. Kamm it is possible that the patterns are Burlington, see, Book one, page 38. Conventional Band. See Book one, page 84. Box in Box. See Book one, page 44. Block Band. See Book one, page 77. Budded Ivy. See Book one, page 111. Cable with Ring (this would seem to be a Design made prior to the opening of the Burlington factory, might have been re-issued), and others, not all pieces with handles (in any of the patterns named) are so marked. The marked pieces may be the output of one man or a chosen few. Careful reading of the Kamm books and the checking of syrup jugs, cream and water pitchers as well as baskets may lead the collector to previously unknown and undentified patterns.

BURLINGTON

BURLINGTON

1. *Cranberry Celery Vase, enamelled flower design.*

2. *Cranberry Thumbprint water pitcher.*

3. *Cranberry and white Swirl design syrup jug.*

4. *Dark blue basket.*

5. *Burlington syrups. Swirl, End-of-day, Thumbprint Swirled line with dot.*

6. *Milk Glass sugar jars.*

BURLINGTON

BURLINGTON

1. Miniature lamp.
2. Bead Swag. Four piece set. (White and yellow opal).
3. Plate. Wilfred Laurier.
   Plate. Victoria Regina.
4. Miniature lamp.
5. Salt shakers. Butterfly and Tassel. Oak Leaf and Inverted Fleur-de-lis. Canadian Moon and Star. Swirl.
6. Salt. Fishscale.
7. Salt Beaded Lattice and Frame.
8. Salt Corn. Note - shakers come in blue, pink, pink, yellow and white opal.

SYRUP JUGS

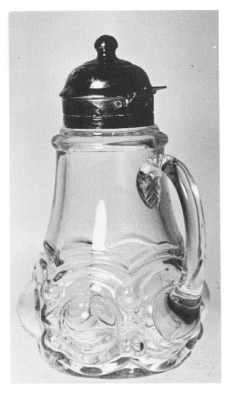

BULBOUS BULL'S EYE

JACOB'S LADDER

BLOCK

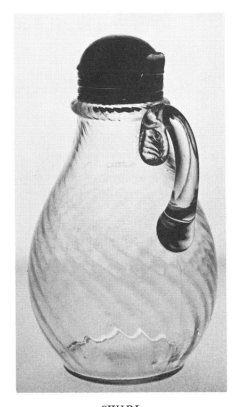

SWIRL

N.S. CROWN

CHANDELIER
SUGAR SHAKER

MANUFACTURERS OF PLATED WARE

Now that more is known of the glass manufactured at Burlington and elsewhere in Canada, the question of silver plated containers, cruets, stands, holders, collars, frames, lids, handles, etc. can be resolved.

Gerald Stevens in CANADIAN GLASS, 1825-1925 suggests that glass objects — if of a quality or composition known to have been produced in a Canadian factory and in silver plated stands, etc., of Canadian origin, i.e. signed by contemporary silversmiths or metal workers, documented as having been active in Canada from 1875 onwards, the glass pieces should be credited to Canada.

TORONTO SILVER PLATE CO. LTD. established prior to 1888

THOMAS FRANCIS, Silversmith, Toronto, Ontario   1869

THOMAS DAVIDSON & CO., Stampers of Tin & Iron Brittannia
    Metal Workers, Coteau Street, St. Augustin, Montreal   1871

OCTAVE GIRARD & BROS., Silver Plated Teasets, Spoons, etc.,
    Three Rivers, P.Q.   1871
    Ontario Charter   1900

SIMPSON, HALL, MILLAR & CO., Montreal   1871

MERIDEN BRITANNIA CO., Hamilton, Ontario   1879

Meriden used several trademarks. One was 'Meriden B Company' in scales. A Meriden catalogue of 1886-87 lists, Double and Triple Cruets, Pickle Tubs, Castors, etc. Types of glass include Cut Glass, Pomona, Art Glass, Coloured Decorated Glass, Gold Inlay, Ruby, Etched (Shamrock design, panelled with embossed bird and branch), Daisy and Button (Russian) (Embossed Stags-Storks-Other Birds), Swirl Cut - pear shaped design like Bohemian overlay.

T. EATON CO., LTD., Meriden manufactured for Eaton's but at the turn
    of the Century, Eaton's used their own trademark. An 'E' enclosed
    in a diamond.

FORBES SILVER CO., TORONTO, Eagle's head mark. This was actually
    the 'Trademark' used by the Meriden Company on their cheaper
    lines after the McKinley Act of 1891.

TORONTO SILVER PLATE CO. LTD.

No. 0108—PICKLE.

Blue, Amber or Crystal Glass.

No. 60—PICKLE.

Amber, Blue, Canary or Crystal Glass.

No. 98—PICKLE.

Blue, Amber or Crystal Glass.

No. 61—PICKLE.

Double.

No. 0118—PICKLE.

Double.

No. 93—PICKLE.

Old Gold, Moss Green, Sapphire or Crystal Glass.

EAGLE SILVER CO., may relate to Forbes, Eagle Rogers. (A William Rogers and International Silver Line)

INTERNATIONAL SILVER CO. OF CANADA. Absorbed many other companies including:

STANDARD SILVER COMPANY, est. 1895

MONARCH SILVER COMPANY, liquidated and became part of Standard Silver Co.

DERBY SILVER

SIMPSON, HALL & MILLAR

WILLIAM ROGERS. NIAGARA FALLS

WILLIAM ROGERS & SON, NIAGARA FALLS

ROGERS BROS. 1847

HOLMES & EDWARDS

FORBES PLATE CO.

Some of these names are 'trademarks' only such as Monarch Silver Company used by Standard Silver Company. But all of these names indicate Canadian-made plated wares.

BENEDICT-PROCTOR, Trenton. Some pieces marked with Benedict over diamond shape.

No. 670—SYRUP PITCHER.

Amber Glass, - $4.50 (Fowler)

CANADIAN GLASS IN CANADIAN SILVER PLATE

1. *Daisy and Depressed Button, Brides' Basket. (amber)*

2. *Beaver topped syrup pitcher (amber)*

3. *Cheese dish (rose, early name for cranberry)*

4. *Beaver topped sardine box (crystal)*

5. *Button Arches dessert set. (green) Note - the spoon is not a matching piece.*

6. *Pickle (amberina)*

Note - With the exception of numbers one and five these items shown in an 1888 catalogue of the Toronto Silver Plate Co. Ltd. These pieces add new vistas to collecting both of plate and glass.

No. 168—CHEESE DISH.

Rose Glass, - - -

No. 1311—SARDINE BOX.

Crystal Glass.

No. 0120—PICKLE.

Amberina Glass.

No. 609—CELERY STAND.

Ruby Glass, - $7.50 (*Futile*)

No. 1568—DESSERT SET.

Rococco Glass, - - $8.00 (*Finesse*)

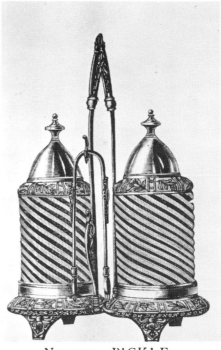

No. 0100—PICKLE.

Double.

S2-148. Pickle Cruet, decorated ruby glass, bright finish, as cut ——— **2.25**

Other styles... ———— **2.50**

Plain ruby glass... **1.85**

Crystal glass.. **1.45 1.65** ————**2.85**

EATON'S 1906 *CATALOGUE*

No. 1571—DESSERT SET.

Rose, Blue or Lemon Glass, Mother-of-Pearl Finish.

Other photographs, Toronto Plate Co.. 1888 catalogue illustrate the various kinds of patterns and quality of glass being used in Canada at that date. It is interesting to note the colours — Blue - Amber - Canary - Ruby (cranberry) -

Old Gold - Moss Green - Sapphire. Patterns shown here include Block - Daisy - Minerva - Sprig - Swirl and a Squared Daisy — note also Burlington handle on No. 1568.

BEAVER FRAME - Five Bottle Castor Set

PALMETTE - Five Bottle Castor Set

PALMETTE - Four Bottle Castor Set

JACOB'S LADDER -
Four Bottle Castor Set

DAISY AND BUTTON —
Six Bottle Castor Set

DIAMOND WITH FAN

BULBOUS BULL'S EYE

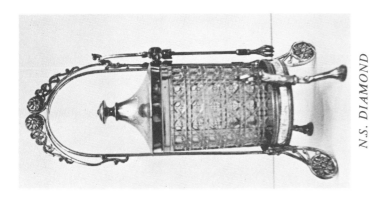

N.S. DIAMOND

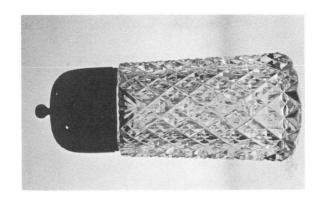

DOMINION WITH FAN

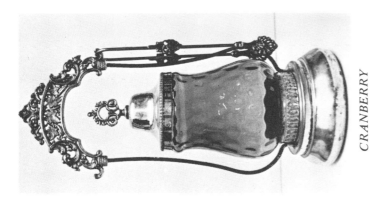

CRANBERRY

WOODROW

CANADIAN

FLOWER AND QUILL

261

GUNDY CLAPPERTON CO. LIMITED
CUT GLASS PATTERNS

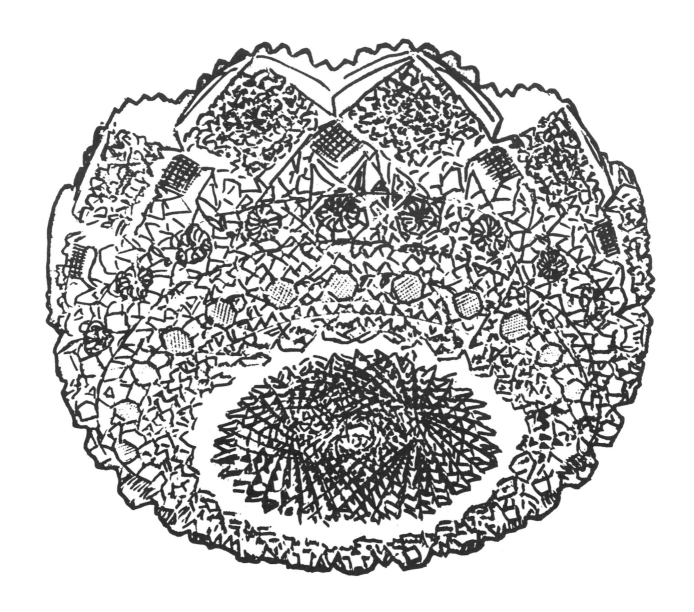

Design 3245

The said Industrial Design consists of a bowl or other vessel of glass having cut in the surface thereof a pattern formed of a combination of the cut commonly known as the hobnail pattern and a border cut of an arrangement of star like patterns cut in substantially diamond shaped panels arranged close to the perimeter of the vessel.

DESIGN 3250

DESIGN 3249

WITNESSES:
E. Heron
A. G. Kelly.
The Minister of Agriculture,
Ottawa, Ont.

All these Designs registered by H. J. S. Dennison. Attorney.

G. H. Clapperton *founded the firm in 1905. Changed the name to Gundy-Clapperton Company in 1906 and continued to use that name for ten or more years — later became Clapperton & Sons Limited and are still in business today.*

Some of their earlier designs are included here-in.
Some of the early pieces are signed with a three-leaf clover containing the initials "G C Co."

Design 3250
The said Industrial Design consists of a bowl or other vessel of glass having deep rounded channels cut into the surface in representation of the braces, leaves and fruit of the Oak, the rounded surfaces being scored with narrow cuts to complete the representation.

Design 3249
The said Industrial Design consists of a bowl or other vessel of glass having the surface thereof divided into a number of

V-shaped sections by recessed channels, known to the trade as panels, said panels being cut into the glass and formed with flat bottoms, said Panels starting at or near the perimeter of a vessel and meeting in the centre of the bottom, the V-shaped sections having suitable designs cut therein.

Design 3443
The said Industrial Design consists of a cut back ground of a general design presenting a plurality of substantially oval pattern giving a general rectangular appearance on the bottom of the bowl or dish and the principal feature of the design consists of the cut representation of a Mayflower and leaves upon an otherwise smooth and clear surface of the glass arranged within the oval portions of the general design.

Design 3888
The said Industrial Design consists of a surface cutting in a ground effect representing a Tulip flower.

OTTAWA CUT GLASS CO. LTD.

DESIGN 3564

DESIGN 3563

DESIGN 3427

Design. 3564. registered. December 19th, 1913.

The said Industrial Design consists of a Butterfly — Leaves cut, called flat mitre, encircling flower called buttercup, composed of four petals, emery worked and each petal filled in with four mitre and one bead cut, centre pi punted and square checkered — each buttercup flower is alternated by a butterfly designed with wings having eight mitre cuts surmounted by six emery worked punties to each wing. Body two bead cuts with three mitre cut feelers.

Design 3563. Registered. December 19th. 1913.

The said Industrial Design consists of a BUTTERCUP leaves out called flat mitre. encircling flower, called buttercup composed of four petals emery worked, and each petal filled in with four mitre and one bead cut, centre punted and square checkered.

The above designs were registered by Frederick R. Perrott, business manager.

Design 3427. Registered March 3rd, 1913.

The said Industrial Design consists of Wild Rose Flower with what is known to the trade as hob star cut in the centre with a bright finish and surrounded by grey cutting known as silver leaf. Leaves and stem in bright finished cut.

This design was registered by Frank Martin of 1188 Wellington St., managing director of the company.

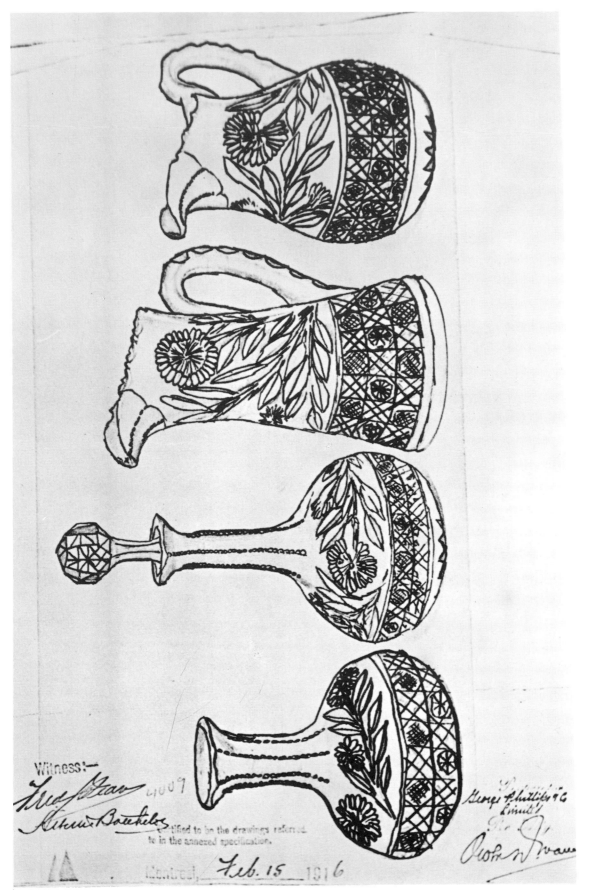

DESIGN 4009

Cut Glass Design 4009 registered February 15, 1916. Design consists of the conventional representation of Carnation Sprays. Registered by Robert A. May, Vice-President, General Superintendent of George Phillips & Co. Ltd.

Old Irish BOWL. *Pattern*

Signed at Toronto, this 9th. day of November,1910,

In the presence of the two undersigned witnesses:

WITNESSES:

OLD IRISH PATTERN

Design 3114

The said Industrial Design consists of a bordered top edge and bottom portion all as per the accompanying facsimile. Old Irish Pattern was the only one registered by the Roden Bros. of Toronto in the years between 1900 and 1915.

LAKEFIELD CUT GLASS

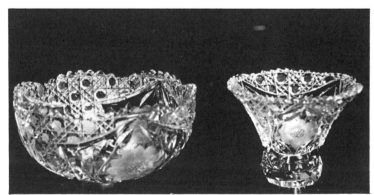

LAKEFIELD CUT GLASS

1. *Cut glass Pitcher 4 tumblers.*

2. *Cut glass Punch bowl on Stand.*

3. *Cut glass Punch bowl stand can be used as Vase.*

Note. Lakefield Cut Glass factory c. 1915-1920 Frank Brown designer, factory employed five glass cutters. Rare pieces are those with the Union Jack, Stars & Stripes and St. George's Cross Flags as the design.

IT HAS BEEN SAID

"Canadians today have become conscious of their interesting past and like to have in their homes some link with it."

Loris S. Russell.
A Heritage of Light.

"Probably the most complicated, beautiful as well as fascinating field of collectables is that phase covering all types of glassware."

Thompson Everingham.
The Treasures All Around You.

"Without glass there would be fewer everyday comforts and luxuries, less knowledge of the world in which we live."
"Today for those who collect old glass, there is in addition the fascination of historical and social significance, for each piece which has survived is tangible evidence of a way of life, of a stage in social and industrial development, and frequently of events which stirred man's emotions."

George S & Helen McKearin.
American Glass.

"Gerald Stevens must be credited with having made the greatest contribution to the study of glass in Canada."

St. George Spendlove.
Collectors Luck.

"Now, the difference in pressed glass pieces may not tell the period to which they belong as certainly as the differences in costume; but there is the same necessity to consider material and design if you wish to determine their age."

Ruth Webb Lee.
Early American Pattern Glass.

"Clues however small could open doors hitherto locked by the passage of time -"

Gerald Stevens.
Canadian Glass. 1825-1925.

"You will sometimes find an example of an unidentified pattern that contains a figure or medallion from one that is well known and fully authenticated."

Hilda & Kevin Spence.
A Guide to Early Canadian Glass.

"With so little known about the manufacture of glass molds we can only assume that American firms supplied both their own and the Canadian market with molds of similar design, which has led to confusion in the collecting of American and Canadian Glass."

George MacLaren.
Nova Scotia Glass.

BURLINGTON PITCHER (Etched)

"In the old glassworks the moulds were fashioned by hand and cast right in the mould-room of the plant, and a mould made in another plant, even if intended as a copy, was never exactly the same."

Hilda & Kevin Spence.
A Guide To Early Canadian Glass.

"It seems reasonably certain that many of the unidentified patterns to be found in shops today will eventually be proven to be of Canadian origin."
"By collecting these unidentified patterns it would be possible to assemble; at lower cost, a collection which would reflect the individuals own imagination, knowledge and taste."
"A few factors that could be considered as guidelines in such an endeavour are age, form or design, colour and perhaps, the relationship of unidentified patterns to known Canadian ones."

John R. Sheeler.
"Collecting Glass in Ontario".
"Antiques in Ontario" 1969 - 70.

"In the field of glass, Gerald Stevens has discovered the ponds, sounded the depths, and located for us some of the magnificent specimens that were present and then he proceeded to share his fishing pole with others that they might not only participate in the fishing with him but, to his delight land some big ones on their own and locate new pools."

John Yaremko.
Canadian Glass c. 1825-1925.

"We all build on the work of our predecessors; as we go on we find a minimum of facts and a maximum of questions."

Alice Hulett Metz.
Early America Pattern Glass.

MAPLE LEAF BOWL (Rare)

GLOSSARY

1. **ANNEALING:**

The tempering by gradual cooling of hot glassware in the lehr (leer). Initial temperature 950 degrees F.

2. **BATCH:**

Raw materials ready for melting in a furnace; melted ingredients ready for blowing, pressing, etc. Temperature for melting 2200 degrees F.

3. **COLOUR:**

Glass is by nature seldom free from colour, traces of iron in the sand produces a greenish tone.

GREEN:

Produced by adding iron.

RUBY RED & TURQUOISE BLUE:

Produced by adding copper

BLUE:

Produced by adding colbalt.

AMETHYST, PINK OR PURPLE:

Produced by varying amounts of maganese.

REDS & PINKS:

Produced by varying amounts of gold.

MILK WHITE (dense opaque):

Produced by varying amounts of oxide of tin.

MILK & WATER (semi-opaque and opalescent):

Produced by varying amounts of arsenic compound or calcined bone.

4. **CRYSTAL:**

More correctly lead glass: Metal made with oxide of lead as the flux. True "Cut" and Crystal glass. Characterized by bell like tone when held by the base and lightly tapped with pencil or flicked (lightly) with fingernail. Heavier than other glass.

5. **CULLETT**

Broken Glass used for the sake of economy and to help fusing. It was sometimes cheaper to purchase broken glass than the ingredients from which the glass was made. Cullet also provided a saving of heat required to melt the batch. A certain percentage was added to every batch.

6. **FINISHER:**

He removed the mould marks from the upper sections of bowls, goblets, pitchers, etc.; a master craftsman.

7. **FLINT:**

Late-nineteenth and twentieth century description for any clear, colourless glass.

7a. **FLINT:**

Glass of lead (flint glass) composed of sand, potash and oxide of lead, sometimes saltpetre was added and oxide of maganese was added to clear the colour and produce the crystal clearness. This glass became most desirable as quality glass. Previously it was believed that such fine glass could only be attained by using silica made from powdered flints (Crystal Glass). Glass termed "Flint" since the late nineteenth century is in fact usually "lime glass". William Leighton of Hobbs, Bruckunier and Company, Wheeling, U.S.A., used bicarbonate of soda, different proportions of lime and other ingredients until he hit on a formula that produced a truly clear glass, almost as bright as lead, not so heavy and having less resonance. This was a tremendous boost to the glass industry for now they were able to produce the look of quality without the cost. The student of glass looks at all pieces with a critical eye and becomes expert enough to tell the difference. Most of what is termed "flint" is in fact "lime" glass. Even some of those pieces so described in the Royal Ontario Museum, Toronto.

Much of the earlier glass made by both American and Canadian factories was the true - glass of lead or "flint" and it is an added thrill to the collector when he finds forms in the pattern or patterns he collects are "flint". Many patterns were made in both "flint" and "lime". If an example in "lime" turns up in a pattern previously considered essentially a "flint" product the authenticity should be checked.

Prices vary according to demand therefore it is not always the quality of the glass that establishes the price but the rarity.

8. **FRIT:**
   Partially cooked and fused ingredients saved and added to a batch.

9. **GATHER:**
   Molten glass removed from the batch at the gathering end of a blowpipe.

10. **GLASS:**
    An artificial compound which is produced by the fusion of silica in the form of sand, flint or quartz, this is done with the aid of an alkaline flux, usually soda or potash. These are the essential ingredients but to produce durable glass, small amounts of other ingredients are added, lime or one of the oxides of lead.

11. **LEHR (Leer):**
    Oven for tempering or annealing glassware.

12. **LIME GLASS:**
    Glass made with soda and lime as a flux, the formula first discovered in 1864. Clear non-lead glass of some brilliance but little resonance.

13. **MARVER:**
    Polished metal or stone slab on which the gather of glass is rolled.

14. **METAL:**
    Glassmakers term for glass in molten or finished state.

15. **POTASH:**
    It is today commercially prepared but early glass makers produced it by burning bracken or beechwood.

16. **SODA:**
    Today made from common salt, previously from the ash of certain marine plants.

17. **WHIMSEY:**
    An object made to demonstrate the skill of the glass blower. Non-commercial objects created for pleasure not profit.

WHO'S WHO

Marion & Douglas Bird:

Authors of the **North American Fruit Jar Index.** Canada's leading authorities in this field of glass collecting.

Thomas B. King:

Co-ordinator of Glasfax, Editor of **Glasfax Newsletter.**

George MacLaren

Chief Curator of History, The Nova Scotia Museum, Halifax, N.S. Author of many books and pamphlets on Nova Scotia furniture, glass and silver. Largely responsible for the creation of the increasingly popular historical museum on Citadel Hill, Halifax.

Max Provick:

Author of **Beausejour's Glass Works,** Canadian (antiques) Collector, January, 1967.

Huia Ryder:

Distinguished authority on furniture and antiques of the Maritimes, author of **"Antique Furniture of New Brunswick".** Lecturer, editor and well known for her former television series on antiques. **The Documented History of New Brunswick Crystal Glass Company** was published by (Mrs..) Huia Ryder in 1962 in the ART BULLETIN, Vol. VI. No. 3. (The New Brunswick Art Department)

John R. Sheeler:

Researcher and collector of Canadiana, with the emphasis on glass. Author of a series of articles in the **"Canadian (Antiques) Collector"** a journal of antiques and fine arts, published monthly. The series entitled **"The Burlington Glass Site"** commenced April, 1968, and some seven or eight articles have appeared since.

Hilda & Kevin Spence:

Brilliant photographers, authors of the most artistic book on Canadian Glass, **A Guide To Early Canadian Glass.**

Gerald Stevens:

Leading authority on Canadiana. His books are considered Canadian Classics and find their rightful place in any library of Canadiana. Well-known as an author and lecturer, Research Associate, Canadiana Department, Royal Ontario Museum. His opinions are respected on both sides of the Atlantic and his columns in Maclean's magazine and Chatelaine eagerly read by fans across the nation.

Azor Vienneau:

Staff artist at the historic branch of the Nova Scotia Museum, Citadel Hill, Halifax. Author of **"The Bottle Collector".**

BIBLIOGRAPHY

Barrett, Richard C. *Blown* N *Pressed American Glass*. The Bennington Museum, Bennington, Vermont, U.S.A.

Belnap, E. M. *Milk Glass*. Crown Publishing Co. 1949.

Bird. Marion & Douglas. *North American Fruit Jar Index* — published by the authors. Orillia.

Haggar, R.G. *Glass and Glassmakers*. Methuen & Co. London, Roy Publishers N.Y.

Haynes, E. Barrington. *Glass*. Penguin Books.

Haynes E. Barrington. *Glass through the Ages*. Richard Clay Co. Ltd.; Suffolk.

Honey W. B. *English Glass*, also *Handbook and Guide to the Museum Glass Collection*. Victoria & Albert Museum Publication. London.

Journal of Glass Studies. An Annual, Published by the Corning Glass Centre. Corning N.Y. (Back issues available)

Kamm. Minnie W. *The Kamm-Wood Encyclopedia of Antique Pattern Glass*. Century House Watkins Glen, N.Y. 2 vols.

Kendrick, Grace. *The Antique Bottle Collector*. Published by the Author.

Knittle, Rhea Mansfield. *Early American Glass*. The Century Co., N.Y.

Lee, Ruth Webb. *Victorian Glass*. Lee Publications. Northboro.

Lee, Ruth Webb. *Early American Pressed Glass*. Northboro, Mass.

Lee, Ruth Webb, *Handbook of Early Pressed Glass Patterns*. Northboro, Mass. Paperbound.

Lee, Ruth Webb. *Antiques & Fakes & Reproductions*.

Lee, Ruth Webb. *Sandwich Glass*.

Lee, Ruth Webb. *Sandwich Glass Handbook*. Paperbound.

McKearin, Helen & George. *American Glass*. Crown Publishers, N.Y.

Metz, Alice Hulett, *Early American Pattern Glass Book I*. Chicago.

Metz, Alice Hulett, *Much More Early American Pattern Glass Book II*. Chicago.

Millard S. T. *Goblets*, Books *One and Two*. Central Press, Kansas.

Millard S. T. *Opaque Glass*. Central Press. Kansas.

Revi. Albert Christian. *American Pressed Glass and Figure Bottles*. Thomas Nelson & Sons, N.Y.

Revi, Albert Christian. *Nineteenth Century Glass*. Its Genesis and Development. Thomas Nelson & Sons, N.Y.

Peterson, Arthur G. *Salt and Pepper Shakers*. Published by the author.

Peterson, Arthur G. 400 *Trademarks on Glass*. Washington College Press. Columbia Union Collection.

Russell, Loris S. *A Heritage of Light*. University of Toronto Press, 1968.

Savage, George. *Glass* — Weindenfield & Nicholson, London, 1965.

Spence, Hilda & Kevin. *A Guide To Early Canadian Glass*. Longman's Canada Ltd., Toronto, Ont., 1966.

Stevens, Gerald. *Early Canadian Glass*. Ryerson Press, Toronto, Ont., 1961. 184 pp. Reprinted in paperback, 1967.

Stevens, Gerald. *In A Canadian Attic*. 1963 — reprinted 1964/65/66/67.

Steven, Gerald. *Canadian Glass 1825-1925*. Ryerson Press, Toronto 1967.

Unitt, Doris & Peter. *Unitt's Canadian Price Guide to Antiques & Collectables*. 1968. Clock House, Peterborough.

Vienneau Azor. *The Bottle Collector*. 1969. Petherick Press, N.S.

MacLaren, George. *Nova Scotia Glass*. Occasional Paper No. 4.

Historical Series No. 1, 1965. Nova Scotia Museum, Halifax. Reprints 1968/69.

MacLaren, George. *Nova Scotia Newsletter*. Vol. 2 and 3, April 1958. Nova Scotia Museum.

Pierce, Lorne. *Early Glass Houses of Nova Scotia*, 1958. Ryerson Press, Toronto.

Pierce, Edith Chown, *Canadian Glass*. A Footnote to History, 1954. Ryerson Press.

Ryder, Huia G. *New Brunswick Glass*, Art Bulletin, Vol. No. 3, 1962. New Brunswick Museum, Saint John, N.B.

PATTERN INDEX

PATTERN INDEX Continued

PATTERN INDEX *Continued*

278

GOBLETS

TREASURY OF CANADIAN GLASS

Second Edition

Comments And/Or Corrections From First Edition

———

Page 15   Include —
EARLY AMERICAN PATTERN GLASS .... Alice Hulett Metz. Metz, Book One

MUCH MORE EARLY AMERICAN PATTERN GLASS
Alice Hulett Metz. Metz, Book Two

Pages 25, 76, 77, 215   CANADIAN DRAPE — better known as GARFIELD DRAPE

Pages 27, 35, 110   CORAL (Fishscale) Tablewares are being included in some collections of Canadiana. Shards of this pattern have not been found. Shards from Burlington are of FISHSCALE lamps only (see page 35).

Page 44   N.S. DIAMOND BIRD FEEDER considered by some collectors to be a match-holder.

Page 46   DAHLIA should read DAHLIA & FESTOON (American).

Pages 65, 220   BEADED GRAPE — Goblet shown is a reproduction.

Page 68   Photo No. 5 includes footed bowl, ht. 6½'', 8¼'' square.

Page 78   Photos No. 1 and No. 2 should read BEADED FLANGE.

Pages 84, 85   CHANDELIER. An inkstand of this pattern was patented by E. B. James. Example seen was stamped "Davis Automatic Inkstand Patented May 8, 1889 E. B. James, Toronto, Canada".

Pages 27, 90, 91   CORINTHIAN. We have seen etched and frosted Corinthian as well as green with opal edge.

Page 96   Photos No. 4 and No. 5 transposed.

Page 154   EARLY NUGGET — Green tumblers are being reproduced.

Page 185   CANE — This pattern included because it was used for inserts in Canadian Silver Plate (pickle, jam and cruet).

Page 214   DIAMOND SUNBURST — Goblet American. The Canadian variant of this pattern shown on Page 12.

Page 279   BEADED OVAL & FAN No. 1 should be No. 2.